Silent Music of Love:
Teach Us to Pray

John O'Brien OFM

Other books by the author

Catch the Wind
Return to Gethsemane
My one Friend is Darkness
Rachel's Tears and Mary's Song
Love Rescue Me
Cry Me a River
Therese and the Little Way of Love and Healing
Clare of Assisi: A living Flame of Love
Waiting for God: From trauma to Healing
With Thee Tender is the Night
Loneliness Knows My Name

To the group of us who met at London Wasps

To Shaun Edwards, Warren Gatland,
Paul Stridgeon (Bobby), Lawrence Dallaglio,
Phil Vickery, Craig Dowd,
Rob Howley, Johnny O'Connor

*"Anyone united to the Lord
becomes one spirit with him"*

(1 Cor 6:17)

Contents

Introduction.. 7

Chapter 1 First Steps 15

Chapter 2 Restless Hearts.. 26

Chapter 3 Looking Unto Jesus 56

Chapter 4 The Canticle of Canticles... 86

Chapter 5 The Divine Canticle of Saint John of the Cross 117

Chapter 6 Two Castles.. 155

Bibliography 169

Introduction

The Believer of the Future:

Karl Rahner (+1984) was an eminent theologian who wrote extensively on God, redemption and the life of grace. One of his most quoted sayings is: "The Christian of the future will be a mystic, or he will not exist at all."[1] Here Rahner does not mean some esoteric phenomenon, but "a genuine experience of God emerging from the very heart of existence." Rahner sees all truly human activity as a free response to God's giving us life and giving us himself.[2] Because our life is a response to God Rahner sees the human being as a mystical one. He says:

"In every human person... there is something like an anonymous, unthematic, perhaps repressed, basic experience of being oriented to God... which can be repressed but not destroyed, which is 'mystical' or (if you prefer a more cautious terminology) has its climax in what the classical masters called infused contemplation."[3]

All human experience is an expression of our acceptance of or rejection of the life of grace. Any experience of goodness or love we have leads us to God who is love (1 Jn 4:8).

"In the final analysis it is unimportant whether you call a personal, genuine, experience of God, which occurs in a deepest core of a human being, "mystical".[4]

---

[1] Karl Rahner, Theological Investigations, XX (New York: 1981) p. 149.

[2] Karl Rahner, Gnade als Mitte menschlicher Existenz: Ein Gespräch mit und über Karl Rahner aus Anlaß seines 70. Geburtstages, in Herausforderung des Christen (Freiburg: 1975), 117-153.

[3] Karl Rahner in Dialogue, edited by Paul Imhof and Hubert Biallowons (New York: 1986), p. 182.

[4] Faith in a Wintry Season: Interviews and Conversations with Karl Rahner in the last years of his life, 1982-1984, edited by Paul Imhof, Harvey D. Egan and Hubert Biallowons (New York: 1990), p. 115.

Mystical theology, or if we prefer 'more cautious terminology' refers to coming to know the presence of God. Our word contemplation translates the Greek word "Theoria" which means "looking at", "gazing at" being aware of the presence of the divine. The English word "contemplation" comes from "con" – and "Templum". The "Templum" (Temple) is the sacred place where God is present. We are temples of the Holy Spirit (1 Cor 6:19). God is everywhere but we lack the spiritual eyes to see him. It is in quietness and trust we find out who we are (see Isaiah 30:15). This is the idea that Rahner had of speaking of the 'mystic'. We come to see God in all things. As Thérèse of Lisieux (+1897) said "All is grace" (Tout est grâce). God is ever at work and planted deep in us is the desire to come to know God and his love.

There are voices that distract us from entering this space. Tina Beattie has written about the new world of atheism.[5] She looks at the work of people like Richard Dawkins, Christopher Hitchens, Sam Harris, Daniel Dennett and others. She tries to show the difference between a scientific view or the world and a theological explanation of the world. The hearer will here come across some of the arguments of both sides. I argue it is when we find the courage to pray and reach out we will sense a divine presence and come to be more human. The words of the Scripture and the great mystics who lived out these words inspire us to discover what these words mean for us. We find ourselves wrestling with the divine. We come to sense the presence of God and we discover the world in us. The Spirit in us is that place where we meet God. We are more truly human inasmuch as we have spirit.[6] Barth means the Holy Spirit. It is the Spirit who brings life to the soul of human beings. Man exists because he has Spirit, because the Spirit grounds and unifies man's body and soul (Barth, op. cit, p. 393). This is the Holy Spirit that we read about in the Acts of the Apostles: "in him we live and move and have our being" (Acts 17:28). Man is and has Spirit because God created us thus. Spirit is the operation of God upon creation and is the principle of man's relation to God (in Barth, p. 355f). We become truly human when

---

[5] Tina Beattie, The New Atheists: The Twilight of Reason and the War on Religion (Maryknoll: 2008).

[6] Karl Barth, Church Dogmatics, III, 2, The Doctrine of Creation (Edinburgh: 1960), p. 366-418.

we are in the Spirit and live and move with him. Human beings are more truly human when they have Spirit. This saying is hard for us because we do not think of 'Spirit'. We are made of material and we see much of our world in terms of utility. We can treat others in the same way. We can define people by their usefulness or otherwise – those we consider useless (not able to make money!) we ignore and judge. Barth's picture of the human person, as being Spirit, or the Spirit in us, is opposed to this view. In God's eyes no person is useless. All have value, God loves all humanity – a lesson we have to learn.

Henri-Louis Bergson:

"Élan Vital" is a term coined by the French philosopher Henri Bergson (+1941) in his 1907 work "Creative Evolution"[7] in which he looked at the question of how things come to be and how things become more complex in their organisation. A distant anticipation of Bergson's idea can be found in the pre-Christian Stoic philosopher Posidonius (+circa 51 B.C.) who postulated a "vital force" emanated from the sun to all living creatures on the earth. The concept of this force (élan vital) is also similar to Artur Schopenhauer's (+1860) concept of the will-to-live.[8]

There were many who disagreed with Bergson (e.g. Julian Huxley [+1975]) who argued that there is no life force (no élan vital) other than the organizational matrix found in the genes themselves. Bergson had moved in a different direction.

As a young man Bergson lost his faith. He was born in Paris of Jewish parents. His father Michael Bergson (+1898) was a Polish Jew, and he was a pianist. His mother Katherine Levison (+1928) was of English and Irish Jewish background. She was originally from Yorkshire. Now at the ages between 14 and 16 Bergson drifted from the faith of his youth. He studied Mathematics and Philosophy. Initially he saw the world as being mechanical and well-ordered. He was also influenced by

---

[7] Henri Bergson, Creative Evolution (London: 1911), translated from the French, original title, L'Évolution Créatrice.

[8] Artur Schopaneur, The World as Will and Representation, 3 vols., (London: 1883-1886).

Darwin. We are just material beings. However as he studied life more and more he began to see how things were more mysterious than he had originally thought. He wrote to Padre Tonquédec in 1912 of how he saw material and memory as being touched by spirit. He saw the world now as having been created and evolution would continue by means of personal consciousness.[9] His spiritual awakening was also fueled by reading the Mystics, those who spoke of their life with God. He said that the mystics had all testified to the fact that God has need of us, just as we need him. The reason he "needs us" is because he wants to express his love for us.[10] He now had a sense of the presence of God. He had thought of becoming a Catholic, but he saw the growing evil of Anti-Semitism, so he remained Jewish so that he could live in solidarity with his brothers and sisters who were suffering daily.

Bergson called Jesus a "super-mystic". He was very moved by Jesus' Sermon on the Mount (Mt 5-7). The love that Jesus had for all humanity was not simply the love of a man for the world. It was the same love with which God loved all humanity. He loved humanity with the very love of God himself.[11] All the mystics witnessed to this divine love which enfolded all things. They lived this love in their daily lives. He said if the words of a great mystic or one of their followers found an echo in our hearts, is it not because in our hearts there is a mystic who sleeps and is only waiting for an occasion to be re-awakened.[12]

Hans Urs Von Balthasar (+1988) lamented the gap that had grown between academic theology and spirituality.[13] He saw 'scientific theology' as being more and more divorced from prayer and had lost the richness of great theologians like Thomas Aquinas and Bonaventure.

[9] Henri Bergson, La Pensée et le Mouvant in A. Robinet (ed.), Henri Bergson, Oeuvres (Paris: 1959) p. 1350.

[10] H. Bergson, Le Due Fonti della Morale e della Religione (Rome-Bari: 1995) p. 222. This book is a translation of Les Deux Sources de la Morale et de la Religion (Paris: 1932).

[11] op. cit., p. 161.

[12] ibid, p. 171.

[13] see H. U. Von Balthasar, Theology and Sanctity, chapter in Explorations in Theology, vol. 1. The Word Made Flesh (San Francisco: 1989) p. 208.

This is helpful on our journey in this book. Thinking about God (theology) is important. It purifies us in our presuppositions. I see theology as being at the service of our life with God. It is something to be done on one's knees. This is the way Von Balthasar saw theology. In the end it is in the human-divine encounter in prayer that we find ourselves and know ourselves in God. In prayer we allow the love of God be poured into our hearts by the Holy Spirit, who has been given to us (see Rom 5:5). The words and lives of those filled with this love can awaken us to our need of this infinite love and in that love find peace. This is the journey I wish to lead the reader on in this book.

Pray, Live and Love

The above words can meet resistance in many hearts. Fear and poor self image can block us from releasing the love that is within us. Abuse, rejection and deep hurt can make us fearful. We are afraid of disappointment. 'The words of the mystics belong to others, not to me' is a common refrain. That is why it takes courage to enter the quietness of prayer. Firstly, we have to make an act of trust and faith. St. John tells us God is love (1 Jn 4:8,16). Jesus is God's word made flesh (Jn 1:14) and his word is love. Even though he was rejected and killed, he still loved all of us. This is why John describes the cross as Jesus' glory. In death he conquered. Love overcame even death and Jesus is alive today extending to all his love, acceptance and forgiveness. In prayer we enter that space of love in the Holy Spirit.

St. Bernard of Clairvaux (+1153) was a Cistercian who meditated much on the Love of God and the struggle to express this love in the face of daily life. He was a man of many talents. He was advisor to the Pope and preached on the need for a crusade. With hindsight this is controversial. He wrote of the experience of being loved. He is a witness to the experience of love in his heart and his teaching helps us find courage to be alone and allow this love find a home in our hearts. We find we are loved, accepted and in this space of prayer we come to know ourselves in God. We "see" with the eyes of faith. "The soul that sees

God sees as if she alone is seen by God" says Bernard.[14] God's love is so vast that it seems to the soul who comes to know him as if that soul were the only person in the world.

This world of love brings us to life and we can begin to organise and see our life as surrounded by love. St. Bernard says:

> Therefore, from what she possesses that belongs to God, the soul in love recognises and has no doubt that she is loved. This is the way it is – God's love gives birth to the soul's love and his prevenient intention makes the soul intent, full of care for him who cares for her. I do not know what closeness of nature it is that enables the soul, when once his face is revealed, to gaze upon God's glory and to be necessarily so quickly conformed to him and transformed into the same image (2 Cor 3:18). Therefore, in whatever way you get yourself ready for God, this is the way he will appear to you.
>
> (Santi Bernardi Opera, 69.7)

In the light of God's love we can come to love ourselves as we are loved. This can lead us to see others as loved by God and in prayer unlock the love that is in our hearts.

St. Teresa of Avila (+1582) begins her classic work "The Interior Castle" by speaking of the dignity of each person. God is at the centre of the soul. He is within and if he were not present we would wither and die (Castle 1,2). For Teresa this presence is a reality. "In him we live and move and have our being" (Acts 17:28). Teresa had her own battle with doubt. She tells us:

> There was one thing of which at first I was ignorant; I did not know that God was in all things, and, when He seemed to me to be so very present, I thought it impossible. I could not cease believing that He was there, for it seemed almost

---

[14] St. Bernard of Clairvaux, Sancti Bernardi Opera (Rome: 1957-1977) 69.8.

certain that I had been conscious of His very presence. Unlearned persons would tell me that He was there only by grace; and so I continued to be greatly distressed. From this doubt I was freed by a very learned man of the Order of the glorious Saint Dominic (Fr. Baron, O.P.): he told me that He was indeed present.

(Life xviii, 15)

The witness of Bernard and Teresa teach us of our infinite dignity in the eyes of God. We are deeply loved and this love can heal and transform us. They belong to a long tradition of mysticism and their teaching is both old and ever new. We are called to accept acceptance and release the love that is in our hearts. We are called to pray, love and live!

Witnesses:

Blessed Pope Paul VI said: "The Virgin Mary and the saints are the luminous reflection and attractive witness of the singular beauty of Christ, the beauty of the infinite love of God who gives himself and makes himself known to men... holiness is a participation in the holiness of God and by it His beauty" (The Via Pulchritudinis, III, 3), and again he says "How can we be credible in announcing 'the good news' if our lives are unable to reflect the beauty of this life" (op. cit, III,3). Modern people are searching for meaning. I have met many agonised souls who bitterly lament the fact that they cannot believe. They are searching for belief, faith and love. They are sceptical of those who preach what they call "the truth" and do not live as they preach. Others have become a scandal for those searching by their conduct and in some cases their abuse. The term "scandal" comes from the Greek word "skandalon" used in the New Testament. It means causing one to stumble. However the searching ones will listen to Christians who practice what they preach.

In the darkness of our world and its sense of loss, the mystics appear as lights to guide us. They lived lives of prayer and sought God. He was the light of their lives. Many have left us their writings. In this work I speak of some of these writing mystics, who give us light in the darkness. They are some of the witnesses Paul VI spoke of.

Unfortunately, many of the great mystics have been generally presented as models of perfection – sometimes too, as internally joyless and ascetical. Yet they were women and men of feeling. They were often insecure and vulnerable and uncertain of the way ahead. For all that, they all shine with a special share in God's holiness and they radiate God's love to us. Each mystic is a masterpiece of the Holy Spirit. The mystics are examples of those who come to know the love of God in their hearts and live their lives in the power of that love. They love all God's people with the very love of God, made possible in them by the Holy Spirit. In reading them we can see our own questions and they reflect to us the transformation that is possible for us. They give us the courage to accept ourselves. We read them to know we are not alone. Their lives and their writings show us that we, too, can share in God's infinite love. We can surrender in prayer to the one to whom they witness.

Chapter One

First Steps:

Gravity is a 2013 science fiction film, co-written, co-edited and co-produced by Alfonso Cuarón. It stars Sandra Bullock and George Clooney as astronauts who are stranded in space after the mid-orbit destruction of the space shuttle, and their subsequent attempt to return to Earth.

Sandra Bulloock plays Dr. Ryan Stone, a brilliant medical engineer on her first shuttle mission, with veteran astronaut Matt Kowalski (George Clooney) in charge of the flight. This is his last mission before retiring. During a routine space-walk, disaster strikes. The shuttle is destroyed leaving Stone and Kowalski completely alone – spiraling out into the surrounding darkness. The deafening silence tells them they have lost contact with earth.

Dr. Ryan Stone (Sandra Bullock) is a researcher and first-time astronaut. She is also a mother who is dealing with the grief after the accidental death of her daughter. In one scene in the film when she finds herself completely alone, she expresses her aloneness in the following way:

> "No one will mourn for me. No one will pray for my soul…
> I'd say one [prayer] for myself but I've never prayed in my
> life… Nobody ever taught me how…"

This scene touches many nerves. In a lot of our experiences in Church there is a lot of talk about God, there is the study of scripture and theology and there are volumes written on complex metaphysical mysteries and Christology. If there is something we do not discuss then we can form a committee to discuss this. Yet there is relatively little time and space given to learning the art of prayer and facing our problems with prayer. Prayer is the oxygen of the spirit and we need this oxygen for life. St. Teresa of Calcutta said "Being unwanted, unloved, uncared for, forgotten by everybody, I think that this is a much greater poverty than the person who has nothing to eat." We cannot be strong alone. Love is not an irrelevant emotion; it is the blood of life. Dr. Ryan Stone knows this loneliness.

In the book of Revelation we read: "And God will wipe away all tears from their eyes; and there will be no more death, neither sorrow, nor crying, neither will there be any more pain, for the former things have passed away" (Rev 21:4). In our world there are many who are dying for a little love. We suffer from a poverty of loneliness. We live in a world where there is a hunger for love, a hunger for God. The picture of God we see in the text for Revelation is a compassionate God. Yet because people (in our case Dr. Ryan Stone) have not learned to pray and have never been taught, they do not know how to let God in and find courage in their loneliness. The cycle continues because they are not transformed by love, they cannot bring love to those around them. The spiral of loneliness continues like our two astronauts spiraling into the surrounding darkness.

Journey to God:

St. Teresa of Avila said in her Life: "mental prayer is in my opinion nothing more than an intimate sharing between friends. It means taking time frequently to be alone with him who we know loves us."[1] It is by loving that we come to know God and by love he comes to us.

St.Teresa's explanation of what prayer is leads us to the problems people have. The first one is that people find it hard to be silent and stay with themselves. Our age and the use of social media keep us from this period of remaining still. All people's troubles derive from not being able to sit in a quiet room alone (Pascal: Pensées, 139). I remember Bruce Springsteen doing an interview about his album 'Nebraska'. He spoke of being alone with himself. He had to find out could he live with himself after he had let those he loved down? Could he live with himself

---

[1] Saint Teresa of Avila, Life 8:5. This definition is used in the Catechism of the Catholic Church, see CCC 4131.

after he had let himself down. Those reflections gave birth to the album 'Nebraska'. His fears of being alone reflect the fears of many who do not enter this space of being alone. They are afraid of seeing themselves and not liking what they see.

Even if people get over the fear of being alone doubt enters the fray. There are those who say God doesn't exist. One such is Richard Dawkins.[2] He is a disciple of Darwin's and argues from biology and evolution that there is no God. One of those who engages with Dawkins is Alister McGrath. He, too, is a scientist. He left religion for a time but came back. In response to Dawkins he set out to construct a theology using scientific reasoning. This appeared in three volumes and was called 'Scientific Theology'.[3] Alister became an Anglican priest and lectures on Divinity.

Another scientist who was a believer was Blaise Pascal (1623-1662). He made important contributions to the study of fluids and clarified the concepts of pressure and vacuum. He wrote in favour of the scientific method. The S.I. unit of pressure is named after him – the pascal. He also did work on calculating machines. A computer language is called after him – Pascal. He also worked on probability theory corresponding with Pierre de Fermat.

In 1624 he had a religious experience. He felt the fire of divine love in his heart. He recorded the experience in a brief not to himself which began: "Fire. God of Abraham, God of Jacob, not of the philosophers and the scholars" and he concluded by quoting Psalm 119:16: "I will not forget thy word. Amen." He kept this writing on a piece of paper he brought everywhere with him. It was only discovered after his death. It was called the "Memorial". Pascal's Memorial reads as follows:

---

[2] Richard Dawkins, The God Delusion (London: 2006).

[3] Alister McGrath, Scientific Theology, 3 vols (London: 2003). He also wrote, The Dawkins Delusion (London: 2007) as a response to Dawkins. Also he can be seen on YouTube in various videos where he debates with Dawkins face to face. One of his other works is The Twilight of Atheism (London: 2004).

The year of grace 1654
Monday, November 23, day of Saint Clement, pope and martyr,
and others in the martyrology.
Vigil of Saint Chrysogonus, martyr, and others.
From about ten-thirty in the evening to about half an hour after midnight.
Fire.
God of Abraham, God of Isaac, God of Jacob, not of the philosophers and savants.
Certitude, certitude; feeling, joy, peace.
God of Jesus Christ. Deum meum et Deum vestrum.
"Thy God shall be my God."
Forgetting the world and everything, except God.
He is only found by the paths taught in the Gospel.
Grandeur of the human soul.
"Just Father, the world has not known you, but I have known you."
Joy, joy, joy, tears of joy.
I separated myself from him: Dereliquerunt me lantern aqua vivae.
"My God, will you abandon me?"
May I not be eternally separated from him.
"This is eternal life, that they know you, the only true God, and him whom you have sent, Jesus Christ."
Jesus Christ.
Jesus Christ.
I separated myself from him; I fled him, renounced him, crucified him.
May I never be separated from him!
He is only kept by he paths taught in the Gospel.

Faith and Reason in Blaise Pascal's "Memorial"
(1935) l Inters.org

This is an historical document. It attests to an event which has a before and an after. It brings to fruition everything experienced up to this point, and fixes a new beginning. The text begins with an exact dating: "1654,

Monday, November…" Even the hour is mentioned: "From about ten-thirty in the evening."

Then comes a series of hastily written words, short sentences, fragments from Holy Scripture, all vibrating with the excitement of a life-changing experience. The first line is formed by a single word "Fire" – "Fire". Two lines below we read

"Certitude, certitude; feeling, joy, peace."

And once again, several lines later:

"Joy, joy, joy, tears of joy."

Pascal has felt the fire of love in his heart. It is an experience of the Holy Spirit. In the "Memorial" there stands the phrase: "Grandeur of the human soul". Even though we are fallen, the fact remains that we are marked by the sign of grandeur.

The feeling of "certitude, joy, peace" is new for Pascal. These are the things he longed for. Now he experiences them in his heart. It is now a reality for him. The reality is luminous and burning: He, as a scientist, put a lot of store in experience. He now experiences the presence of the living God.

Then comes this interesting phrase:

"God of Abraham, God of Isaac, God of Jacob,
not of the philosophers and savants, the God of Jesus Christ."

It is not the God we find in thought and logic that Pascal speaks of. He has really known the love of God poured into his heart by the Holy Spirit (Romans 5:5). In the letter to the Ephesians Paul says that "You may be able to comprehend, with all the Saints, what is the length, height and depth of the Messiah's love" (Eph 3:18). Pascal knows in his heart "the love of God which is beyond all understanding" (Eph 3:19).

God is a person and he is love (1 Jn 4:8,16). In Jesus God comes to us. God is the God of Jesus Christ. When Philip asks, "Lord, show us the Father", Jesus answers, "Have I been with you so long, and yet you do not know me Philip? He who has seen me has seen the Father" (Jn 14:9). The Christian God is the God of Jesus Christ, the one Jesus calls Father.

A little note, written later, has come down to us. It expresses with great power the experience of newness of life, of the new order of existence. It is found in fragment 793.

> "The first thing that God inspires in the soul which he deigns to truly touch is a quite extraordinary knowledge and power of sight (vue) through which the soul considers things and itself in a completely new way.
>
> This new light causes it fear, and brings it an anxiety which traverses the repose which it used to find in the things which delighted it. It can no longer enjoy with tranquility the things which used to charm it. A continual scruple combats it in this enjoyment... But it finds still more bitterness in the exercises of piety than in the vanities of the world. On the one hand, the presence of visible objects affects it more than the hope of invisible ones, and on the other, the solidity of the invisible ones affects it more than the vanity of the visible ones. And thus the presence of the ones and the solidity of the others excite its affection, and the vanity of the ones and the absence of the others excite its aversion, so that there arises within it a disorder and a confusion..."

What appears in the experience of the Memorial is a new beginning. The old forms and the new forms of consciousness mix with one another and struggle with one another. It is in this way that Pascal grows into his new life with God. His work, "Pensées", shows us how he grew through this struggle.

Pascal's work on religion, referred to posthumously as the Pensées (Thoughts) was not completed before his death. It was an examination and defense of the Christian faith. One of Pascal's sayings was: 'Love has reasons which reason cannot understand' (Pensées, part 2, no. 277). This means that we are not intellect alone. We are beings with emotions. We desire love and to be loved. This points to another reality. We can say if love exists, then God exists. In the third part of the Pensées we have the famous Pascal wager. Basically the wager says that a rational person should live as though God exists and seek to believe in God. If God does not actually exist, such a person will only have a finite loss (some pleasures, luxuries etc.) whereas they stand to receive infinite gain (as represented by eternity in Heaven) and avoid infinite losses (eternity in Hell).[4] Pascal centers his argument for God's existence on love. He is deeply influenced by his experience of love recorded in the 'Memorial'. Pascal's lonely genius did not belong to any particular school of thought. He said "Je suis seul" (I am alone). He sought the truth where it was to be found. For him theology is essentially conversation with God as the gracious Thou, who before all else gives with love the true knowledge of the Thou. Theology (and prayer) is necessarily dialogic and existential (Pensées, 602).

Fyodor Dostoyevsky (1821-1881) wrote about a different form of atheism in "The Brothers Karamazov" (1879-1880), the atheism born out of protest. Dostoyevsky saw that our basic need is to be loved and accepted. Yet in a world that is often cruel many are denied this love and acceptance. Ivan Karamazov is shocked at the world's cruelty and the absence of God. He speaks about a young girl who is abused and beaten by her family. She is locked away. She cries out in prayer to God but he doesn't seem to hear. She would not be interested in our theories of good and evil. She is in too much pain. Then Ivan tells Alyosha, his younger brother, about the horrific death of a young boy by a sadistic landowner. Alyosha too finds it difficult to find a reason for such cruelty. Then in chapter 5 of book 5, Ivan tells the parable of the 'Grand Inquisitor', set in Spain during the time of the Spanish Inquisition. He controls the people by burning heretics and by giving the people enough food. Then Jesus the Christ comes to his world in Seville. He heals the people but the Inquisitor has him arrested. He tells Jesus that 'free-will' was a mistake because people were not able to make good choices. They must

---

[4] Blaise Pascal in Columbia History of Western Philosophy (Columbia: 2006) page 353.

be controlled by a dictator. So Jesus must die. The parable ends when Jesus kisses his tormentor. The Inquisitor feels a surge of tenderness, but quickly controls it and orders Jesus' execution. After the parable, Alyosha kisses Ivan. 'Plagiarism' says Ivan.

In The Brothers, Alyosha is taught by the monk Zosima. After Zosima's death Alyosha leaves the monastery. He is to go into the world of people bringing light where there is darkness. In a dream he hears the reading of the wedding feast of Cana and he knows he is to go and change the water of existence into the joy of Christ. Dostoyevsky knew this struggle between good and evil in himself. When he was a political prisoner in Siberia he felt a surge of despair. He turned his face towards the wall. Among the prisoners this meant he had given up. The cruelty and sadism of the camp had beaten him. He tells the story in the "Diary of a Winter" for February 1876. As he slept came the memory of an incident that happened many years ago when Dostoyevsky was a child of five. He was out walking in a field when he thought he heard a wolf howl. In his panic he ran and found Marei, a serf, who was ploughing a field. Marci comforted the boy and told him to cross himself to obtain protection. 'But I did not cross myself', writes Dostoyevsky, 'the corners of my lips quivered; and I believe, that was what impressed him most. Slowly he stretched out his thick thumb, with the black nail soiled with earth, and gently touched my trembling lips ... and he looked at me with a long motherly smile.' And now, twenty years later, it was Marei's soil-blackened thumb that Dostoyevsky particularly remembered:

and if I had been his own son he could not have bestowed upon me a glance full of a more serene love. And yet, who had prompted him? He was a peasant serf, while I was a nobleman's son. No one would find out how he had caressed me and no one would reward him. The meeting was a solitary one, in an open field; and only God, maybe, perceived from above what a profound and enlightened human feeling, what delicate, almost womanly tenderness may fill the heart of some ignorant Russian peasant serf. And when I climbed down off my bunk and gazed around I felt I could behold these unfortunate men with a wholly different outlook, for suddenly, by some miracle, all the hatred and anger had completely vanished from my heart.

That is a classic illustration of the melting of the heart which is essential if one is to see one's fellow human beings in the light of the Holy Spirit. and the fact that Russians have a special word for such a moment – *umilenie* – is in itself testimony to the frequency with which they have been alert to those moments throughout the long history of the Russian people's spiritual endeavour. That moment of *umilenie* in 1852 gave an impulse to the spirit of Dostoyevsky that was to sustain him for the rest of his life throughout many trials and failures.[5]

Dostoyevsky learned from Marei. He had rediscovered Christ. In his work 'The Brothers Karamazov' Ivan rebels against the world order. He rejected God who, according to Ivan, demanded the tears of an innocent child. His rebellion leads to madness. His philosophy ends with Smerdyakov, his half-brother, when Smerdyakov kills Ivan's father, Fyodor. Alyosha decides his vocation is to wipe the tears for the suffering ones (and especially children). He sees all the suffering ones as being invited to the banquet of love. Dostoyevsky was shaken by the words he put into Ivan's mouth. Ultimately he looked to the figure of Christ to guide him and transform him and, in the end, society: He wished to promote concept called '*sobornost*'. This can be described as a communion in the name of Christ. This communion is not a mechanical communion but a spiritual communion where all people will be gathered 'in a great, universal, brotherly fellowship in the name of Christ'. In the kingdom every tear will be wiped away and there will be no more pain.

Love Is:

St. Teresa of Avila in her description of prayer (see above) speaks of a prayer as an intimate sharing between friends and spending time with the one "whom we know loves us". So often we do not love ourselves.

---

[5] Donald Nicholl, Triumphs of the Spirit in Russia (London: 1999) p. 151.

In the Gospel of Luke, when Jesus calls Peter, Peter responds "Go away from me Lord, for I am a sinful man" (Lk 5:8). Yet he discovers Jesus loves him even when he is all out of love with himself.

In the Gospel of John we read: "No one has greater love than this, to lay down one's life for one's friends." (Jn 15:13). Jesus did this to bring us, his friends, into his heart. Karl Barth (+1968) was once asked in an interview what was the basis of his theology. He said simply, Jesus loves me. "I know because the Bible taught me so". He was using the words of an old hymn. We show ourselves as friends when we let God's love in and share it with others (see Jn 15:14). In the letter of John we read: "See what love the Father has given us, that we should be called children of God and that is what we are" (1 Jn 3:1). We are the friends of Jesus and sons and daughters of the Father. We have a unique identity in this. St. Teresa begins her work "The Interior Castle, Chap. 1" by reflecting on the fact that we are made in the image and likeness of God (see Gen 1:26-29). However we are now alienated from God and our true selves. God loves us and when we let ourselves be loved then we enter into communion with God. This is the journey in the "Interior Castle". "Beloved we are God's children now… what we know is, when he is revealed, we shall be like him because we shall see him as he is" (1 Jn 3:4). This is the interior transformation that takes place.

"Beloved, let us love one another, because love is from God; everyone who loves is born of God and knows God. Whoever does not love does not know God because God is love" (1 Jn 4:7-8). This is the very nature of God. We are loved and accepted. The love we receive on earth is often only partial. Sometimes we receive the opposite of love and we are devastated. We expect the same from God but we find he is different. He loves us truly without any partiality. He accepts us wholly. It takes courage to move from our experience of imperfect love and non-acceptance to one where we are loved totally and accepted fully. God is greater than our hearts (see 1 Jn 3:19-22) and he abides in those who keep his commandments (see 1 Jn 3:23-24). His commandments are summed up in the words: "Love one another as I have loved you" (Jn 13:34). Jesus the Christ has shown us God's love (1 Jn 4:7-12). Not only is God's love revealed in Jesus, but now this love must be revealed in the Christian and the Christian community, which can help us through love (see Jn 5:26, 6:57, 1 Jn 5:11). St. Teresa's description of prayer means we can love God (because he has loved us first [1 Jn 4:19]) and we can let ourselves be loved. Transformation in the world begins when people are loved and healed, and start investing in other people.

St. Teresa writes in "The Book of Her Life": "I beg... that we may all be mad for love of him who for love of us was called mad" (Life 16:6). Jesus, to show us his love, suffered the cross and hell. We are truly loved and part of our journey is to allow that love enter our hearts.

Chapter 2

Restless Hearts:

St. Augustine (365-430 A.D.) began his Confessions with the words: "You have made us for yourself, O Lord, and our hearts are restless until they rest in You." Behind Augustine were a succession of desperate searches for fulfilment, excessive pleasures, false religions, dissipation and distraction. He found no happiness. It was when he came to know God and his revelation in Jesus that he found the peace he longed for. His conversion began when he read this passage from Paul's letter to the Romans:

> "Let us live decent lives as people do in the daytime: no drunkenness, no promiscuity or licentiousness, and no wrangling or jealousy. Let our armour be the Lord Jesus Christ."
>
> (Rom 13:13f) [Confessions, viii,7].

Many feel Augustine's "restless heart". We seek love and yet end up in strange places. Many seek for something, but cannot find a connection with the one we call God. Prayer is a common, ubiquitous human practice. It is the human reach towards holy mystery and divine intimacy.

In the Gifford lectures, given by J. Wentzel van Huyssteen, he speaks of Upper Paleolithic cave drawings in Southwest Europe.[1] The cave drawings are early attempts to make contact with a world beyond human control, and reached out beyond what they knew. He suggests, following the work of David Lewis-Williams, they may be seen "as a membrane or veil between people and the spirit world", and that leads Van Huyssteen to say that the essential elements of religion are "wired into

---

[1] J. Wentzel van Huyssteen, Alone in the World? Human Uniqueness in Science and Theology (Gifford Lectures: Grand Rapids, 2006) p. 168-215.

the brain".[2] In Judaeo-Christian prayer, Israel in the Old Testament, prays to the God of Exodus who is the creator of heaven and earth. Therefore Israel prays in a certain way to this God who reveals himself. Israel groaned to the Lord and he heard their plea and he rescued them from slavery. In Exodus we read:

> "The sons of Israel, groaning in their slavery, cried out for help and from the depths of their slavery their cry came up to God. God heard their cry and he called to mind his covenant with Abraham, Isaac and Jacob. God looked down upon the sons of Israel..."
>
> (Ex 2:23-25)

In a more modern recent work by Lindsey Crittenden, "A Skeptic Learns to Pray", she gives an account of her opening conversation with an Episcopal priest as she faced the violent loss of her brother.

> Lindsey: But I'm a mess... I feel awful.
> Priest: God doesn't mind... Have you tried prayer?
> Lindsey: I don't know how.
> Priest: Yes you do. You just admitted you feel [awful]. That's a start.

She goes on:

> "I'd been crying out 'Help' in the car and underwater in the swimming pool, where no-one could hear. Desperation that blatant and raw felt embarrassing but oddly liberating and justified too."[3]

Israel's prayer was like that. They, as slaves, expressed a deeply felt cry for help. They hoped to find a life beyond what they had. As they prayed they did not know if they would be heard, but they prayed. Their cry rose to God and their voice is heard. God, whose name is Yahweh,

---

[2] ibid, 251, 259.

[3] Lindsey Crittenden, The Water Will Hold You: A Skeptic Learns to Pray (New York: 2007) p. 18.

comes to them. The Israelite cry for help to one they do not know. God answers and tells Moses his name is YHWH (which we write as Yahweh) (Ex 3:1-12). God promises to be with Moses when he goes to the Pharaoh to ask him to let God's people go (Ex 3:12). Psalm 83 is a prayer in this spirit. The persons praying pour out their needs to God:

"O God, do not remain silent;
do not be unmoved, O God, or unresponsive!
See how your enemies are stirring,
see those who hate you raise their head."

(Ps 83:1f)

The psalmist is confident he is heard. In Psalm 18 we read

"In my distress I called to Yahweh
and to my God I cried:
From his temple he heard my voice,
my cry came to his ears."

(Ps 18:6)

Israel finds God is by nature compassionate (hannan). The word merciful (rahum) is said of God alone. It is his nature to be so. In Exodus we read of Moses' exchange with God as he led the people out of Israel.

He [Moses] called on the name of Yahweh. Yahweh passed before him and proclaimed, 'Yahweh, Yahweh, a God of tenderness and compassion, slow to anger, rich in kindness and faithfulness...' And Moses bowed down to the ground and worshipped. "If indeed I have found favour" he said, "Let my God come with us. True, they are a headstrong people, but forgive us our faults and our sins, and adopt us as your heritage."

(Ex 34:6-9)

In our time we are on a journey to get to know this God and by our prayer allow him to enter our lives.

Lectio Divina - Hearing God's word:

The Second Vatican Council document on Revelation tells us:

"...and let them remember that prayer should accompany the reading of sacred Scripture, so that God and human beings may talk to each other for when we speak to him we pray; we hear him when we read the divine saying"[4]
(Dei Verbum, no. 25).

Prayer and reading are two moments or components of the one event. Praying and reading the Scripture becomes a dialogue. God is present in his word and he is present to us in our hearts. Hearing his word leads us deeper into his world and we learn to live in his love. The message of the sacred texts historically relates to events in the past. The sacred books, at the same time, have a timeless quality, like a work of art. When we listen the words become real for us today. For instance in the prophet Isaiah we read: "...you are precious in my eyes, because you are honoured and I love you" (Is 43:4). This was said to a people once but it shows God's true nature and applies in all times to those who hear these words and pray. By the power of the Holy Spirit these words have a meaning for us today.

Dei Verbum also tells us: "'The obedience of faith' (Rom 16:26 see 1:5, 2 Cor 10:5-6) is to be given to God who reveals, an obedience by which human beings commit their entire selves to God, offering the full submission of intellect and will to God who reveals,"[5] ...To make this act of faith, the grace of God and the interior help of the Holy Spirit, must precede and assist, moving the heart and turning it to God, opening the eyes of the mind and giving "joy and ease to everyone in assenting to the truth and believing it."[6] Moreover He confirmed with divine testimony what revelation proclaimed, that God is with us to free us

---

[4] First Vatican Council, Dogmatic Constitution on the Catholic Faith, chapter 2, "On Revelation", Denzinger 1786.

[5] cf Second Council of Nicaea, Denzinger 303.

[6] Council of Trent, session IV, Decree on Sacred Canon, cf First Vatican Council, Dogmatic Constitution on Faith and Reason, chapter 4, Denzinger 1800.

from the darkness of sin and death, and raise us up to life eternal [Dei Verbum no. 5]. The word 'obedience' comes from the Latin "ob" - "audire" which means "from hearing". The Holy Spirit is with us to help us hear the word of God anew today. He mediates God's presence to us. When we listen and pray we are in the presence of the divine. We are also gifted by the Spirit with a role to play in cooperating with God and playing our part in the healing of the world and its people. Therefore through this praying, reading and study of the sacred books "the word of God may spread rapidly and be glorified (2 Thess 3:1) and the treasure of God's word may enter our hearts and heal us." (see Dei Verbum, no. 26). God, who spoke of old, still speaks to us through his word (see Dei Verbum 8). The God who is not distant is present in his word and these words are the vehicle for a loving encounter between God and his beloved children [see Dei Verbum, no. 2].

There have been many practices in the Church of reading and praying the "word". This was called "Lectio Divina" in the monasteries and we are re-discovering this way of praying today. Lectio Divina is a Latin term and means "divine reading". It is a traditional Benedictine practice of scriptural reading, meditation and prayer. We enter into communion with God. Scripture is to be studied, yes! However study is at the service of prayer. God's word is a living word and is real for us today. The word of God can lead to an intimate sharing between friends, God and us. We can be alone with him and through his word and deeds we learn how much he loves us. Our Lectio involves a constant movement between study, listening, commitment and living.

Basil Pennington, O.C.S.O., wrote the following about Lectio Divina:

One of the most amazing statements in the Bible – and there are lots of amazing statements in the Bible – are those words of Jesus to us: "I no longer call you servants, but friends." This is almighty God speaking, the Lord of all creation. And God says it to you and to me: "Friend." Friend! What is more wonderful, more precious than a true friend, one who is there for us? One with whom we can share anything and everything, one with whom there is full communion and communication. Our communication with our Divine Friend needs to be a two-way street. And if we are smart, we let God get in the first word. This is precisely what lectio divine is: letting our Divine Friend speak to us through an inspired and inspiring Word. Lectio is meeting with a very special Friend who is God; listening to God, really listening; and responding in intimate prayer and in the way we take that Word with us and let it shape our lives.[7]

The quotation about us being called friends is from John 15:15. In the Gospel of John Jesus is God's word made flesh (Jn 1:14) and in the letter of John we read that God is love (1 Jn 4:8,16) and his word to us is love. We are his friends, the ones he loves. In the Gospels the ministers of the word are eyewitnesses (Lk 1:2). The word is not just what Jesus said but the mystery of God revealed in Christ (Col 1:25ff). Jesus calls us to love one another as he loves us (see Jn 13:34). His love reveals the Father's love and this love is real today for us. This love is eternal.

God's Love in Christ Jesus

God's love is a love that pardons. This love leads us to forgive others. Love for others is love for Jesus (Mt 25:31ff). We are called to repentance, make a commitment to God and thus create a new people who will tread the way of self-sacrificing love that Jesus lived. A point of interest is that Mark calls Jesus beloved at the beginning both of his ministry (Mk 1:11) and his passion (Mk 9:1). Paul sees this situation clearly. He speaks of God's love revealed in Jesus. Paul says of Jesus: "In his body lives the fulness of divinity" (Col 2:9). This is his way of saying that God speaks through this man Jesus. In Romans Paul speaks of those who are in Christ Jesus. "In" Christ for Paul means our communion. When we are in union with Christ we become one in spirit with him (see 1 Cor 6:17).

---

[7] M. Basil Pennington, Lectio Divina: Reviewing the Ancient Practice of Praying the Scriptures (New York: 1998) p. xi.

The reason, therefore, why those who are in Christ Jesus are not condemned, is that the law of the spirit of life in Christ Jesus has set you free from the law of sin and death. God has done what the Law, because of our unspiritual nature, was unable to do. God dealt with sin by sending his own Son in a body as physical as any sinful body, and in that body God condemned sin. He did this in order that the Law's just demands might be satisfied in us, who behave not as our unspiritual nature but as the spirit dictates.

(Rom 8:1-4)

"In" Christ Jesus means we are in union with him and now we leave a former way of life behind. Once we were "flesh" and dominated by sin and alienation (Rom 5:16-18). We are now led by God's Spirit. We are now new people through Christ's death, resurrection and the giving of the Holy Spirit. God sent his own son to give us life: He was sent "in the form of human flesh." He came in a form like ours in that he experienced the evil of this fallen world and suffered death (see Gal 3:13). In suffering this way and by his resurrection he takes away the power of sin (cf Gal 1:4).

Paul's argument in 1:1 leads to a hymn to Christ's love for us and then to the assurance of God's love in Christ (Rom 8:28, 31f).

After saying this, what can we add? With God on our side who can be against us? Since God did not spare his own Son, but gave him up to benefit us all, we may be certain, after such a gift, that he will not refuse anything he can give. Could anyone accuse those that God has chosen? When God acquits, could anyone condemn? Could Christ Jesus? No! He not only died for us – he rose from the dead, and there at God's right hand he stands and pleads for us. Nothing therefore can come between us and the love of Christ, even if we are troubled or worried, or being persecuted, or lacking food or clothes, or being threatened or even attacked. As scripture promised: For your sake we are being massacred daily, and reckoned as sheep for the slaughter. These are the trials through which we triumph, by the power of him who loved us.

For I am certain of this: neither death nor life, no angel, no prince, nothing that exists, nothing still to come, not any power, or height or depth, nor any created thing, can ever come between us and the love of God made visible in Christ Jesus our Lord.

(Rom 8:31-39)

God's eternal love is Christ's love (Rom 5:8; 8:37). In this passage attention is placed on the resurrection of Jesus. This Jesus is alive and intercedes for us. Nothing can take us away from the love of Christ and the Father. This love is eternal and unchanging. Paul quotes Ps 44:23, which bemoans the injustice done to the faithful, but at the same time recalls the steadfastness of God's faithfulness to his people. The Psalmist calls:

"Wake up, Lord! Why are you asleep?
Awake! Do not abandon us for good.
Why do you hide your face,
and forget we are wretched and exploited."

(Ps 44:23f)

Yahweh hears and sends his son Jesus to be with us. This Jesus died but by God's power rose again and is with us today by the power of the Holy Spirit. God is faithful and loving. No power can take away God's love. Only our rebellion can take us away, but God continues to love us. In the end when we are in Christ Jesus, nothing can separate us "from the love of God in Christ Jesus." The love of God revealed in Christ Jesus forms the basis for Christian life and hope. God's new community in Christ Jesus is filled with the active and compelling power of God's love. This love has "been poured into our hearts by the Holy Spirit given us" (Rom 5:5). He goes on to say: "We were still helpless when at his appointed time Christ died for sinful men... what proves that Christ loves us is that Christ died for us while we were still sinners" (Rom 5:6-9). We are reconciled with God in the power of the Spirit. God's love for us is one with his mercy (Sir 18:11), wisdom (Sir 1:9) and "grace" (Ps

45:3). The giving of the Spirit to us means God's presence is mediated to us. He is really present to us today. Paul goes on to speak in 5:6-9 about Jesus dying for us and this really demonstrates the depths of God's love in Jesus for us. By the power of the Holy Spirit we come to know we are accepted, loved and forgiven. It is not easy to die, even for a just man, but Jesus gave his life so that we may have life and as John says in his Gospel "have life to the full" (Jn 10:10). All these texts can form the basis for Lectio Divina. The words transcend history and are as real today as they ever were. The words are addressed to us. By prayerful meditation we discover the love of God revealed in Jesus. This love is for you and for me. In time this love can break down our barriers. We can be healed and transformed. We can become one with Jesus and become one in Spirit with him (see 1 Cor 6:17). By the power of the Holy Spirit we come to know and experience the love of God. By his power we can be healed. Also in this power of the Holy Spirit we can bring love to others. We can learn compassion for ourselves and others. We are a new creation (see 2 Cor 5:17).

Our Search for God:

Deep inside us is our longing for love, acceptance, ultimately for God. By contemplating people like Augustine we come to share his quest for meaning, we can relate his story to ours. We met Augustine at the start of this chapter. Augustine was born in 354 in the Roman provincial town of Thagaste in what is now Algeria. His father, Patrick, was a pagan and his mother, Monica, a devout Christian who brought Augustine up in the faith. At the age of about seventeen Augustine went off to Carthage (in modern Tunisia) to study rhetoric at the university there. He fathered a son out of wedlock. He was drawn towards Manichaeism – a dualist religion positing a cosmic conflict between the forces of good and evil, light and darkness. This seemed a more mature religion than his mother's faith (Confessions III.VI.10). This influenced his spiritual life for about a decade. Augustine moved to Rome in 383 to set up a school of rhetoric. A year later he accepted a professorship in Milan. By this time he was disenchanted with his Manichaeism and he was attracted to the philosophy of the Neo-Platonists.

At the same time he fell under the influence of Milan's bishop, Ambrose, whose sermons Augustine admired both for their content and style.

> So I came to Milan, to the bishop and devout servant of God, Ambrose, famed among the best men of the whole world... All unknowing I was brought by God to him, that knowing, I should be brought by him to God. That man of God received me as a father.
>
> (Confessions, V, XIII.23)

In 386 he thought he heard a child's voice saying "take and read" (Tolle e lege), and he read part of Paul's letter to the Romans (Rom 13:3). This is Augustine's own account of his conversion:

> And suddenly I heard a voice from some nearby house, a boy's voice or a girl's voice, I do not know: but it was a sort of sing-song, repeated again and again, 'Pick it up! Read! Pick it up! Read!' ... Damming back the flood of my tears I arose, interpreting the incident as quite certainly a divine command to open my book of Scripture and read the passage at which I should open... So I was moved to return to the place where Alypius [his closest friend and witness to the events] was sitting, for I had put down the Apostle's book there when I arose. I snatched it up, opened it, and in silence read the passage upon which my eyes fell: 'Not in dissipation and drunkenness, nor in debauchery and lewdness, nor in arguing and jealousy; but put on the Lord Jesus Christ, and make no provision for the flesh or the gratification of our desires' (Romans 13:13-14). I had no wish to read further, and no need. For in that instant, with the very ending of the sentence, it was as though a light of utter confidence shone in all my heart, and all the darkness of uncertainty vanished away.
>
> (Confessions, VIII.XII,29)

He converted to Christianity and was baptised by Ambrose in 387. He returned to north Africa and set up a quasi-monastic community in

Thagaste. In 391 he was visiting the town of Hippo Regius on the coast when the local people pressed him to become a priest and in 396 he became bishop of Hippo, a position he held for the next thirty-four years. As well as his pastoral work as bishop he was also a prolific writer. He wrote his Confessions as a reaction against the Donatists. This movement had its roots in the persecutions of the Christians under Diocletian. They would not accept back into the Church those who had apostasised. They were rigorists. For them the Church must be a Church of saints. Augustine wrote to show the wider audience of Christians that there was mercy and forgiveness from God. He knew this because he had experienced this himself. His aim was pastoral.

In 413 he began work on 'The City of God' which he continued to work at until 426. Two years later the Vandals invaded North Africa and by 430 were laying siege to Hippo. Augustine died at this time. He had seen the fall of the Roman Empire (the earthly city) but he pointed out that the eternal city ("eternal" life in God) endures. This 'city' is one that lasts.

Transformed by Love:

Jean-Paul Sartre once said that we become self-aware through the eyes of another. It is in relationship that we become ourselves. Augustine in his Confessions showed that it was in a relationship with God that he became who he was called to be. In this he found the peace he was looking for. He believed that God is always near to us – he is closer to us than we are to ourselves. He recalls the time of his "past foulness" not to linger there but to appreciate more the love he received: "For love of thy love do I,… recalling my most vicious ways that thou mayest grow sweet to me – Thou sweetness without deception" (Confessions II,I.I). He longed more for the adulation of men than life with God. In this way Augustine showed the mercy of God in the face of our rebellion. Finally it was in relationship with God that Augustine could become other-centred than self-centred. Augustine had abandoned God, but God never abandoned him (Confessions VI,V.8). He comes to laugh at the person he was and the things he wanted (Confessions I,VI.8). Relationship with God made him free.

In this way Augustine led us to see another important part of prayer. Initially we concentrated on God's word to us. Now in Augustine we see the human person placed before the word of God and therefore God himself. He shows us his rebellions and failures. In this way we can see our own failures and lack of love. He comes to praise God for his goodness: "Let my heart and my tongue praise you and let all my bones say, 'Lord, who is like you'" (Confessions, IX, I.I.). Without this love Augustine had tied himself in knots (Confessions, II,X.18). With God there is peace and he who enters into communion with God finds joy (ibid.).

It is in the 'heart' that we come to know God. The heart is a scriptural theme and we find it in the work of Gregory of Nyssa (+394 A.D.). The 'heart' can be thought of as the personal centre of the human being. The heart is the vibrant essence of the person. It is when we come to this part of ourselves that we come to know ourselves as we really are.[8] It is in silence and trust we enter our centre and there we meet God. When Augustine calls on God he comes to realise that God lives in the heart (Confessions, I.II.2). It is we who find ourselves 'outside' away from our hearts. In silence we allow ourselves enter this space and meet God who is closer to us than we are to ourselves (see Confessions, III,VI.II). Augustine recalls that "You (God) were within, and I was in the world outside, and sought you there" (Confessions X,XXVII.38). God is the source, origin and end of all human desire.

In so many of our lives we find we do not really love ourselves. It is easier than one thinks to hate oneself (Bernanos). Our experiences of unloving and abuse can lead to self-loathing and doubt. Augustine tells us that God loves us as we are. His love is total and perfect. His acceptance of us forms the basis for our self-acceptance and transformation. Etty Hillesum (+1943) speaks of her journey to self-acceptance. Instead of the word "heart", she speaks of a "deep well": "There is a deep well inside me. And in it dwells God. Sometimes I am there too. But more often stones and grit block the well, and God is

---

[8] see A. Maxsein, Philisophia Cordis Das Wesen der Personalität bei Augustus (Salzburg: 1966) p. 14.

37

buried beneath. Then he must be dug out again."[9] it is when we allow ourselves to go deep we find God lives at the centre of our being. The 'stones' and the grit Etty speaks about are the blocks we have – our fears, anxieties and false images of God. We need to come to terms with these and allow God to be God. John Climacus (+649) tells us: "Be of good heart. If passions rule over us, let us with great confidence offer to Christ our spiritual weakness and our impotence ...He will help us irrespective of what we deserve on the sole condition that we descend continually to the bottom, into the abyss of humility."[10] Our addictions, faults and wounds might discourage us, but God in Christ is bigger than our addictions, faults and wounds and we can cast all these into his hands because he loves us. St. Peter tells us: "Cast all your anxiety on him because he cares for you" (1 Peter 5:7). As Etty points out, this is something we must undertake again and again and at the end rest with the one who loves us more than we do ourselves. God teaches true self-compassion and opens our hearts to treat others with the same compassion. In Antoine de Saint-Exupéry's "Le Petit Prince" (The Little Prince), the prince tells the stranded pilot: "One sees with the heart. What is essential is invisible to the eye." This is the central theme of the book.[11] This complements what we read in Augustine and what Etty Hillesum calls the deep well within us.

One of the Fathers of the desert said "Go, sit in a cell, and your cell will teach you everything" (Abba Moses). Jesus showed us when he took time away to be by himself the value of solitude. In solitude we meet a Presence that is always with us and in silence we welcome that Presence. Robert Kull is an American who moved to Canada. He left his job to experience solitude and see what he could learn.[12] Initially he was consumed with fear before the vast darkness. He called on his higher power: "In that moment I felt lifted and found myself floating in a pool of clear light. Looking down, I sensed myself lying peacefully on the

[9] Etty Hillesum, An Interrupted Life (New York: 1996) August 25, 1941.

[10] John Climacus, Ladder of Divine Ascent, quoted in Olivier Clement, The Roots of Christian Mysticism (New York: 1993) p. 152.

[11] see Laurent de Bodin de Galembert, Idée, Idéalisme et Idéologie, Dans les Oeuvres Choisies de Saint Exupéry (Thesis: Université Paris IV, 2000) p. 13.

[12] Robert Kull, Solitude: Seeking Wildness in Extremes (Novato, Ca.: 2008).

forest floor. The world was no longer a hostile, alien place."[13] Kull shares his experience of being alone. A Christian of the last century said "If you enter into the silence, you risk meeting God." Kull left his forest retreat and went to a remote island off the coast of Chile, where he spent a year alone in the Patagonian wilderness. Kull moved towards Buddhism but he still used the word 'God'. He wanted to "explore through living, the physical, psychological, emotional and spiritual effects of deep wilderness solitude."[14] He tells us at times "the mind and the heart are all over the place, from the most trivial and mundane and negative to the joyful, peaceful and sacred. Solitude is like the rest of life, only with less opportunity to escape into diversion."[15] Kull's journey is one many are reluctant to take. We come to see ourselves in all our frailty and vulnerability. We escape spending time alone by seeking diversion. If that doesn't work we seek diversion from diversion (T.S. Eliot). Kull abandoned himself to solitude and did find moments of peace. When Augustine points to the journey to the heart it is by embracing solitude that we discover, on the one hand, who we are and on the other hand we discover we are loved and accepted by God. His love is there to heal us and make us new. In solitude we meet our own loneliness, lack of love and the times we have let others and ourselves down. In meeting God we begin to move towards self-compassion and a new way of living. We know our weaknesses and fragility and we reach out for strength to the one who is closer to us than we are to ourselves.

A feast of friends:

In the garden in Milan, Augustine, in the midst of his spiritual crisis was accompanied by a friend, Alypius. Not only was he a witness to Augustine's conversion, he was the first to benefit from Augustine's compassion (see Confessions VIII,XII.30). In Augustine's journey to faith he never journeys alone. There are always people who are there for him and they have their part to play in Augustine's life. Augustine

[13] ibid, p. xiv.
[14] ibid, p. 214.
[15] ibid, p. 103.

recalls the death of a friend who he had brought into Manichaeism. He is shattered. He tells us:

> "He died and I was not there. Black grief closed over my heart and wherever I looked I saw only death. My native land was a torment to me and my father's house unbelievable misery. Everything I had shared with my friend turned into hideous anguish without him. My eyes sought him everywhere, but he was missing..."
>
> (Confessions: IV,VIII.9)

As Augustine tells us of his grief he also introduces us to hope: "He alone loses no-one dear to him, to whom all are dear in the One who is never lost" (Confessions IV,IX.14)

Another and vital part of his life was his mother Monica (+387). She suffered in her marriage but all the time she prayed for her son Augustine and trusted in God. Her prayerful life accompanied her son. Before her death Monica and Augustine were together in a garden in Ostia. They sensed that God was present with them and they felt love in their hearts.

> As the *flame of love burned* stronger in us and raised us higher towards the eternal God, our *thoughts* ranged over the whole compass of material things in their various degrees, up to the heavens themselves, from which the sun and the moon and the stars shine down upon the earth. Higher still we climbed, *thinking and speaking* all the while in *wonder* at all that you have made. At length we came to our own souls and passed beyond them to that place of everlasting plenty, where you feed Israel for ever with the food of *truth*. There life is that *Wisdom* by which all these things that we *know* are made, all things that were, have been and all that are yet to be. But that *Wisdom* is not made. It is as it has always been and as it will be forever or, rather, I should not say that it has been or will be, for it simply is, because eternity is not in the past or in the future. And while

we *spoke* of the eternal *Wisdom*, *longing* for and *straining* for it with all the strength of our *hearts*, for one fleeting instant we reached out and touched it. Then with a sigh, leaving our spiritual harvest bound to it, we returned to the sound of our own *speech*, in which each *word* has a beginning and ending, far different from your Word, our Lord, who abides in himself for ever, yet never grows old and gives new life to all things.[16]

For Augustine in this passage the words relating to the mind (thoughts, thinking, speaking and word) and the words signifying heart (love, burned, wonder, longing, straining) work together. "Love is itself a form of understanding" (St. Gregory the Great).

The journey to coming to know God and ourselves, as we are, in the eyes of God is a graced journey. We are always in the hands of God. The Scriptures, and the reading of and hearing of, were very important in the life of St. Augustine – the very first words of the Confessions (I:I:1) are from Psalm 47:2: "You are great, Lord, and worthy to be praised". The final words of the Confessions are a paraphrase of Mt 7:7, a text close to Augustine's heart. This text reads: "Ask, and it will be given to you; seek and you will find; knock and the door will be opened to you" (Mt 7:7; NIV). With the Confessions he speaks of his hunger for the Psalm (IX;IV:8), until in Books 11-13 we find him lovingly reflecting on the Genesis account of creation, relishing each word and savouring the account he finds there: "May your scriptures be my pure delight, so that I may not be deceived in them and do not lead others astray in interpreting them" (Confessions X:II,3). He allows the scriptural words become his own.

The figure of Christ in whom God was totally present was central to Augustine. He is the one mediator between God and humanity, "Jesus Christ himself human" (1 Tim 2:5). He says in another place: "You're not yet here. You're still on the way... Where are we going? To Christ.

[16] see Stephen Chase, Contemplation and Compassion: The Victorine Tradition (London: 2003) p. 83f. He emphasises in italics certain words that point to the experience of Monica and Augustine. The quote is from Confessions IX,X.1

How do we get there? Through Christ" (Ennarrationes in Psalmos 123:2). For Augustine John's Gospel gave him an inexhaustible narrative that could speak to the depths of the human heart. He was very struck by the image of the beloved disciple resting his head on the bosom of Jesus. He speaks of pressing our own hearts against the Word (Ennarrationes in Psalmos 21:11:19). The Word made flesh is Jesus himself (Jn 1:14). The words of God and God in Jesus delight and transfigure the human heart suggest another Christological title for Augustine. He suffered from bad health all his life – Augustine points out we are willing to trust doctors but we do not trust God! Christ is humanity's saving medicine.

> How much doctors do against the will of their patients, and yet they are not doing it against their health. The doctor sometimes makes a mistake, God never. So if you entrust yourself to a doctor who can make mistakes sometimes, you are entrusting yourself to human treatment – and not just for dressing which is soothing, or some bandaging which doesn't hurt you, but very often it is for him to burn, to cut, to remove a limb that was born with you and for you, that you entrust yourself to him. You don't say, 'What if he has it all wrong and I will be minus one finger!' You allow him to cut, in case it should infect your whole body. And you won't allow God to operate upon you, to amputate some of your wealth [he is preaching here about trusting God in the face of financial loss!]
>
> (Sermon 15A.8)

The healing power, programme and practice of Christ the physician are repeatedly brought before Augustine's listeners as he lays out for them what he calls God's 'medicinal saving economy – dispensatio medicinalis' (Iohannis epistulam tractatus 36.4); God's 'healthcare programme' for humanity is Christ who is doctor and medicine and health itself.

> You who are sick take heart, look to your doctor, can you still be without hope? The afflictions were great, the

wounds incurable, the illness fatal. You pay attention to the magnitude of the disease, aren't you going to pay attention to the omnipotence of the doctor? You are desperate, but he is omnipotent. The apostles are his witnesses, the first ones healed now proclaim this doctor. Yet even they were healed more in hope than in realisation.

(In Epistulam Iohannis, 8.13)

St. Augustine speaks about Mt 25:31-46. This is the passage where Jesus identifies with the sick, those in prison or in need. When we give to any of these we give to Jesus himself. The passage reads:

'When the Son of Man comes in his glory, escorted by all the angels, then he will take his seat on his throne of glory. All the nations will be assembled before him and he will separate men one from another as the shepherd separates sheep from goats. He will place the sheep on his right hand and the goats on his left. Then the King will say to those on his right hand, "Come, you whom my Father has blessed, take for your heritage the kingdom prepared for you since the foundation of the world. For I was hungry and you gave me food; I was thirsty and you gave me drink; I was a stranger and you made me welcome; naked and you clothed me, sick and you visited me, in prison and you came to see me." Then the virtuous will say to him in reply, "Lord, when did we see you hungry and feed you; or thirsty and give you drink? When did we see you a stranger and make you welcome; naked and clothe you; sick or in prison and go to see you?" And the King will answer, "I tell you solemnly, in so far as you did this to one of the least of these brothers of mine, you did it to me". Next he will say to those on his left hand, "Go away from me, with your curse upon you, to the eternal fire prepared for the devil and his angels. For I was hungry and you never gave me food; I was thirsty and you never gave me anything to drink; I was a stranger and you never made me welcome, naked and you never clothed me, sick and in prison and you never visited me." Then it will be their turn to ask, "Lord, when did we see you hungry or thirsty, a stranger or naked, sick or in prison, and did not come to your help?" Then he will answer, "I tell you solemnly, in so far as you neglected to do this to one of the least of these, you neglected to do it to me". And they will go away to eternal punishment, and the virtuous to eternal life.'

Mt 25:31-46

St. Augustine comments on this passage in the following way:

...it is by loving that one becomes a member of Christ, becomes through love incorporated into the body of Christ; and there will be the one Christ loving himself... when therefore you love a member of Christ, you're loving Christ, you're loving the Son of God; when you love Christ, you're loving the Son of God, when you love the Son of God you love the Father. Love can never be separated. Choose for yourself what you love and the rest will follow.

(epistulam Iohannis tractatus, 103)

This insight into the oneness and wholeness of Christ is matched by a call to a oneness and wholeness in our love. It was nourished by his intense engagement with the psalms, which he understood to be the voice of Christ speaking. If the psalms are the voice of Christ, they speak not only Christ's solidarity with us and our solidarity with him but also our solidarity with one another.

The whole church is made up of all the faithful, because all the faithful are the members of Christ. Thus our Head [Christ] dwells in heaven from whence he governs his body, and while we are separated in terms of vision, we are united in terms of love. Thus the whole Christ is head and body and so in every psalm we hear the voice of the head and the voice of the body. He did not want to speak in a separated way because he did not want to be separated. He says: 'Behold I am with you always until the consummation of

44

the world.' If he is with us, he speaks in us, he speaks concerning us, he speaks through us; and accordingly we speak in him and indeed we speak the truth because we speak in him. But when we want to speak in our own name and out of our own voice [and not Christ's], we remain in untruth.

(Ennarrationes in Psalmos, 56.1)

We must reach out to the poor and suffering, bringing with us the consolation, help and healing we have received (see 2 Cor 1:1-4). St. Augustine speaks of his journey to coming to know God and Jesus:

"Late have I love you,
Beauty so ancient and so new,
Late have I love you!
Lo, you were within,
but I outside, seeking there for you,
And upon the shapely things you have made
I rushed headlong,
I, misshapen.
You were with me but I was not with you,
They held me back from you,
those things which would have no being
were they not in you.
You called, shouted, broke through my deafness;
You flared, blazed, banished my blindness;
You lavished your fragrance,
I gasped, and now I pant for you;
I tasted you, and I hunger and thirst;
You touched me, and I burned for your peace."

(Confessions X;XXVII,38)

The Image of the Trinity

In Gen 1:26 we read that God made human beings in his own image and likeness. This was an important theme for Augustine and the early Latin

Fathers. Augustine saw the central theme of spirituality as the revelation of the image of God in human beings. For some of the Fathers the image (imago) signified the link between God and the intellectual nature he created, while the likeness (similitudo) was that which was lost through original sin, but was capable of being regained through the grace of Christ. In the original Genesis account the terms used in Hebrew are selem and demuth. Selem (imago) is more permanent but demuth (likeness) is more fleeting. This should not be pressed too far. Image points to form and structure, physical or spiritual, while likeness refers to the idea of resemblance and outward structure. The nature of human beings is that we are made in the image of God and our character is potentially divine. The fall tells us we are far from living our true dignity.

Augustine said "man was made to be the image of God in that part of his nature, wherein he surpasses the brute beasts, that is of course his reason, or mind, or intelligence, or whatever we wish to call it" (Commentary on Gen 3. 20. 30). The idea of image is found in his work 'The Trinity'. He begins his work with the following prayer:

"Grant the power of finding you to the one you created to find you, and to whom you have more and more given the hope of finding you. May I remember you, understand you, love you. Increase all these things in me until you reform me fully."

(The Trinity, 15.28.51)

In book 8 he speaks of love. He says: "...if you were able to perceive goodness with all other goods removed, you would perceive God; and if you cleave to him in love, you will be immediately made happy "(8.3.5). The problem is "that in order to enjoy the presence of him from whom we are, we must remain steadfast in relation to him and must cleave to him." (The Trinity, 8.4.6). It is possible through grace to have knowledge of God. Love of our neighbour is love of God. Love flows from one to another. Our life of love is grounded in God who is love (1 Jn 4:8). All our love is grounded in the inner life of Father, Son and Holy Spirit. Our coming to know ourselves is the source of the mind's love of itself. "There is an image of the Trinity: the mind itself, and its knowledge which is its offspring and the word which comes from it. Love is the third. And these three are one and are substance" (The Trinity, 9.12.18). The operation of the mind is an image of the Trinity. It is the memory, intellect and will that is the image of the Trinity. The memory, in Augustine's time, is what we would call personality. The intellect is an expression of the personality, the 'Word' in the Trinity and it is the will which is the place of love that is the image of the Holy Spirit. In writing 'The Trinity' Augustine tried to open the interior eye, the eye of the soul, to the work of the Trinity in the soul and through grace have the inner person renewed and transformed to become true 'images' of God. The whole purpose of human beings created as 'image' of God is to attune ourselves more consciously and more directly to our heavenly source:

> Hence this trinity of the mind is not on that account the image of God because the mind remembers itself, understands itself, and loves itself, but because it can also remember, understand and love him by whom it was made. And when it does so, it becomes wise; but if it does not, even though it remembers itself, knows itself, and loves itself, it is foolish.
> (The Trinity 14.12.15 [PL 42:1048])

Augustine continues to warn us that the activity of reforming the 'image' by deepening our awareness of the Trinity will never be completed perfectly in this life: "When the vision of God will be perfect then there will be a perfect likeness to God in the image" (The Trinity, 14.17.23). The process of transformation begins now, in this life.

Augustine believed that the reform of the 'image' of God could not be accomplished without grace. He saw the intervention of "the mediator of God and humanity, the man Jesus Christ" (1 Tim 2:5). Because Jesus the Christ is truly divine and human he functions both as the goal of our journey and as our way there. Augustine said "...It is his godhead toward which, his humanity which, we make progress (Homily on John, 42:8). Jesus is the word of God made flesh (Jn 1:14) and God speaks to us in his son. This is a theme Augustine develops in his Sermons on John. We are united with Jesus and his saving work takes place within us.

> "It is clear that because he said that humans are gods they are deified from his grace not born from his substance... He who justifies also deifies, because by justification he makes sons of God... If we have been made God's sons, we have also been made gods; but this is by adopting grace, not by nature giving birth."
>
> (Hom. on Ps. 49.1.2 [PL 36:565])

Augustine speaks of 'deification' – he means by this we are the adopted children of God in Christ. Jesus the Christ is the one who makes it possible for us to be the people we are called to be. 'Deification' is a reality begun in this life and will only be fully complete when we enter Heaven. In the first letter of St. John we read:

> "Think of the love the Father has lavished on us by letting us be called God's children and that is what we are... my dear people, we are already the children of God, but what we are to be in the future has not yet been revealed; all we know is, that when it is revealed, we shall be like him because we shall see him as he really is."
>
> (1 Jn 3:1-4)

It is in Christ's body, the Church, that we journey towards the Father of mercies.

The love with which God first loved us (1 Jn 4:14) enters our hearts by the Holy Spirit. The heart must be healed before we can see God with 'the eyes of faith'. This healing is the work of the Holy Spirit, who is Love itself. The Holy Spirit is the bond of love between Father and Son. Love is the 'glue' by which we cling to whatever we truly desire (The Trinity 2, 10.8.11) and charity is the true glue that binds us to God (Homily on Psalm 62.17). Augustine spoke of union in terms of the bond that knits all believers together into the one 'Body of Christ', the Church. It is here we are united with Christ, for Augustine. Here he uses

Paul's teaching about the mystical body, all believers united in Christ (see 1 Cor 12).

In 1 Cor 12 Paul explains how we, all together, make up the body of Christ which is his Church. We are all given gifts to build one another up. He speaks about the variety of gifts that are given:

> There is a variety of gifts but always the same Spirit; there are all sorts of service to be done, but always to the same Lord; working in all sorts of different ways in different people, it is the same God who is working in all of them. The particular way in which the Spirit is given to each person is for a good purpose. One may have the gift of preaching with wisdom given him by the Spirit; another may have the gift of preaching instruction given him by the same Spirit; and another the gift of faith given by the same Spirit; another again the gift of healing, through this one Spirit; one, the power of miracles; another, prophecy; another the gift of recognising spirits; another the gift of tongues and another the ability to interpret them. All these are the work of one and the same Spirit, who distributes different gifts to different people just as he chooses.
>
> (1 Cor 12:4-11)

All the gifts have a common origin in the Holy Spirit and are meant for mutual upbuilding. There are other lists of gifts (Rom 12:6-8, Eph 4:11). Since all gifts are gifts of God we should be humble and acknowledge God as the source of all good.

Against the boasting of the Christian community Paul goes on to emphasise our unity in Christ:

> Just as a human body, though it is made up of many parts, is a single unit because all these parts, though many, make one body, so it is with Christ. In the one Spirit we were all baptised, Jews as well as Greeks, slaves as well as citizens, and one Spirit was given to us all to drink.

Nor is the body to be identified with any one of its many parts. If the foot were to say, 'I am not a hand and so I do not belong to the body', would that mean that it stopped being part of the body? If the ear were to say, 'I am not an eye, and so I do not belong to the body', would that mean that it was not a part of the body? If your whole body was just one eye, how would you hear anything? If it was just one ear, how would you smell anything?

(1 Cor 12:4-17)

Paul spoke of "body" to explain the organic unity of the Church. He was well aware that divisions occurred in Christian communities but he used the idea of body to focus our minds on being less selfish and more open to the needs of others. There is diversity in the people called, but we should be united in love. The Spirit is found in the Church (see 1 Cor 3:16,6:19). In the Spirit there is a diversity of gifts and members just as there are different parts of the body. All are called to work together. Each person is unique and has their own contribution to make. These are the ideas Augustine used in his teaching about the Church.

Speaking about our needs:

The psalms have provided a rich treasury of prayer for countless generations. We saw this in Augustine. Many of us were trained to be always polite in our prayers. The language of the psalms becomes very disconcerting for Christians who consider themselves too holy for the words of the psalms. However the psalms are the word of God and they teach us how to pray. In the first part of the psalm the psalmist pours out his pain or feelings. He does not apologise for what he says. If he is feeling sad he expresses this. Here we find the importance of the psalms. The psalmist trusts God and the words of the psalm form a sacred space where the psalmist meets God. He hands over to God all he feels, trusting that God is bigger than his complaints or feelings, and in reaching out to God he awaits God's answer. If for instance the person praying feels irritated, they express in trust their negativity. Then they await God's reply. It might come in the form of a scripture verse, for instance, in Romans 12:10 we read: "Do not take revenge, my dear friends, but leave room for God's wrath, for it is written: 'It is mine to avenge; I will repay' says the Lord." Here Paul quotes Leviticus 19:18.

The psalmist hears the voice of God and in the light of God's love he changes to do God's will.

Psalm 63 speaks of the excellence of God's love and our hunger to discover this love. The superscript says that the psalm is associated with David's stay in the Judean wilderness. This can be either during his escape from Saul (1 Sam 23) or in a later period from Absalom (2 Sam 15:13-30). Its spirit is close to that of Ps 42:1-2 and fits in well with Psalms 61 and 62. These psalms are bound by a common closeness and they seek fellowship with God.

> A psalm of David. When he was in the desert of Judah
> "O God, you are my God,
> for you my soul is thirsting,
> my body pines for you,
> like a dry weary land without water,"
>
> (Ps 63:1)

He yearns for fellowship with the Lord. He is like one who thirsts for water after days in the desert. There is a sense of thirst and fatigue like that of someone alone in the desert. The dry, arid climate saps one of strength. He seeks love yet many of us are fearful before true and pure love. There have been so many betrayals and so much abuse that we become fearful and lacking in trust. This is the desert so many find themselves in. We make excuses to keep a safe distance between ourselves and others, and ultimately God. Yet deep down we long for love and in praying these words of the psalm we open up for ourselves the possibility of finding this love we long for. The phrase in the psalm "my body pines for you" is derived from the Hebrew root [s-h-r] which is the same root as the word of dawn. The psalmist hopes for a new dawn – as do we who pray with him.

"So I gaze on you in the sanctuary,
to see your strength and glory.
For your love is better than life,
my lips will speak your praise."

(Ps 63:2-3)

The search for God arises from the psalmist's past experience of fellowship and experience of God's goodness. He remembers God's holiness, power, glory (Hebrew: kabôd) and love (hesed). Isaiah had a vision of God's holiness and glory (Isa 6:3). By reading and praying Isaiah's text we come to know God's glory. The temple is a symbol of God's presence. The word "contemplation" has as its root the word "templum". This is where we find the presence of God. Contemplation means viewing, looking at and gazing in love at the presence of God. This is where we find peace. We acquire the courage to accept we are loved.

The psalmist's yearning for God is heightened by the past experience of fellowship. This can be the experience of others (e.g. Isaiah) and by contemplating their words we can share their experience. The God who was present to the prophet and the psalmist is present to us. In praying out the words of the psalm we call on God to let us know again he is with us. In truth God is always with us but, like Augustine, we are not with him. In prayer we heal the blocks we have placed before God. One time St. Francis (+1226) was tempted to doubt God's love. This is a common temptation for God's friends. Evil tries to destroy this special friendship between God and his beloved:

As the merits of saint Francis increased,
his quarrel with the ancient serpent also increased.
The greater his gift,
the more subtle the serpent's attempts,
and the more violent his attacks on him.
Although he had often shown himself to be
a might warrior
who had not yielded in the struggle even for an hour,
still the serpent tried to attack
the one who always won.

At one time a very serious temptation of spirit came upon the holy father, surely to embellish his crown. Because of it he was filled with anguish and sorrow; he afflicted and chastised his body, he prayed and wept bitterly. He was under attack in this way for several years, until one day while praying at Saint Mary of the Portiuncula, he heard in spirit a voice: "Francis, if you had faith like a mustard seed, you would tell the mountain to move from here, and it would move." The saint replied: "Lord, what is the mountain that I could move?" And again he heard: "The mountain is your temptation." And he said, sobbing: "Lord, be it done to me as you have said!" At once the whole temptation was driven away. He was set free and inwardly became completely calm.

(2 Celano 115)

In Matthew 17:20 we hear Jesus say "…if your faith were the size of a mustard seed you could say to this mountain, 'Move from here to there', and it would move; nothing would be impossible for you." The Holy Spirit brought this text to the mind of Saint Francis. The mountain was the doubt he had and he knew in faith he could tell this "mountain" to leave. He found peace in God by the power of the Holy Spirit. God's love is better than life and gives life.

> "So I will bless you all my life,
> in your name I will lift up my hands.
> My soul shall be filled as with a banquet,
> my mouth shall praise you with joy."

(Ps 63:4-5)

"My soul thirsts for you" now becomes "my soul is satisfied" (v.5). The Hebrew words for "fat", the choicest parts of a sacrificed animal offered to God according to ritual practice (see Lev 3:14-16) lie behind this psalm. He now shares in a banquet God has prepared for him, a banquet of very rich food. The mood changes because the psalmist feels in faith that his prayer has been answered. God is with us now in the prayer and we share a celebration of love. We discover that love is better than life.

"On my bed I remember you,
On you I muse through the night,
for you have been my help,
in the shadow of your wings I rejoice,
Your right hand holds me fast."

(Ps 63:6-8)

The psalmist now sings for joy because of the healed relationship. This is a joy that transforms the hours of darkness and searching. His anxieties have been replaced by contemplating the love of God. This God is now present to the psalmist. The words of the prayer lead him into the very heart of God. The psalmist clings to the presence. "In the shadow of your wings" the psalmist finds refuge. This reference is found in Pss. 17:8 and 36:7 also. It is a reference to the cherubim whose wings stretched over the centre of the ark, the symbol of God's presence with his people. This is the God who now protects the psalmist and we who pray this psalm. We form a worshipping community to celebrate this love.

"Those who seek my life will be destroyed,
They will go down into the depths of the earth.
They will be given over to the sword,
and become food for jackals.
But the king will rejoice in God;
all who swear by God's name will praise him,
while the mouths of liars will be silenced.

(Ps 63:9-11)

The wicked had plans to destroy the righteous (see Pr 3:25) but ended up destroying themselves. The psalmist takes delight in the plight of the wicked. It is only when we can acknowledge, as the psalmist does here in prayer, our vindictiveness before God that we can hear God calling us in Jesus to love our enemies, to bless those that curse you, and to do good to those who hate us (Mt 5:44). Only when we are honest before God can we let in his love which heals and transforms us. In the last verse the king rejoices in the Lord. This catches an aspect of healing we have forgotten. St. Seraphim of Sarov (+1833) said that when one soul finds peace a thousand are saved. The healing of one person draws others into the healing and this becomes a source of joy for all. We are more inclined to think in an age that we are just individuals and isolated one from the other. The psalms remind us that we all have an effect, one on the other and when we find healing and peace we do affect others. They are drawn into that sacred space where healing occurs. This psalm grew out of worship. When we worship with others we feel the impulse to pray.

> "Public worship draws out the latent life in the human spirit. Those who, when alone, do not, or cannot pray, find an impulse to pray when they worship with others, and some will pray together who cannot pray alone, as many would sing in chorus who would not sing solos. Many who are spiritually weak find spiritual strength in a common spiritual effort."[17]
>
> (Siddur Lev Chadash, p. 7)

So the psalmist joins with the worshipping chorus, "I will bless you as long as I live" (see Ps 16:7). He also says in other psalms: "I will lift up my hands (Ps 28:2) and "call upon your name", celebrating the true character of God (see Ps 5:11) who is kind and full of compassion. When one person is healed, many are healed. The psalmist in Ps 63 celebrates his finding God and the worshipping community celebrate with him because they are led once again to find God and then healing in his light.

---

[17] see Siddur Lev Chadash: Services and Prayers for Weekdays and Sabbaths, Festivals and Various Occasions (Union of Liberal and Progressive Synagogues: London: 1995) p. 7.

Chapter 3

Looking Unto Jesus (Heb 12:2)

The disciples of Jesus could look at him and see he was very special. "One day Jesus was praying in a certain place. When he was finished one of his disciples said to him 'Lord, teach us to pray as John taught his disciples'" (Luke 11:1). Jesus introduced them to the Our Father (Luke 11:2-4) and Jesus then taught them by parables to be constant in prayer (Luke 11:5-13). Mark in his Gospel tells us of Jesus praying in the morning and at night (Mk 1:35 and 6:46) after he had dismissed the crowds. Jesus also prayed before making his most important decisions. He prayed before his baptism in the Jordan (Lk 3:21), at the moment of transfiguration (Lk 9:25), before electing the twelve (Lk 6:12), before Peter's confession at Philippi (Lk 9:18), before he completed a miracle (see Mk 6:41, 7:34, 8:6-7, Jn 11:41-42). He also prayed at the meal before his passion (cf Jn 17) and also, as we shall see, in Gethsemane and on the Cross.

The Prayer of a Son:

"...a voice from heaven said, 'This is my Son, whom I love, with him I am well pleased'" (Mt 3:17). This is the scene in Matthew's Gospel where a voice from heaven is heard expressing God's love for Jesus. It comes after Jesus' baptism in the Jordan by John. In Jesus' prayer he showed himself aware of his special relationship to God. He calls God Father ('Abba' in Aramaic). The word 'Abba' is used by a child for its father. Jesus often sought out quiet places so he could be with God. One example is Luke 6:12: "Now it was about this time that he went out into the hills to pray; and he spent the whole night in prayer to God. When day came he summoned his disciples and picked twelve of them..." (Lk 6:12f). Jesus "separated himself" from his disciples. The sense of the original Greek emphasises the fact that Jesus went away to be on his own. He entered into solitude, a space where he could be with God his father. Jesus prayed as a man. The Greek word *"dianukteuon"* tells us that Jesus spent the whole night in prayer. Jesus needed this solitude where he was filled with the presence of his father. He valued the times where he could pray and be one in the Spirit with his Father. In Mark's account of Gethsemane Jesus calls God "Abba" (Mk 13:34). This shows the intimate union of Jesus with God his Father.

Paul uses the expression "in Christ". This can have a general meaning but there are other cases when this has a particular subjective meaning. It means our union with Jesus. Examples of Paul's usage of this term are: "You must reckon yourself dead indeed to sin and alive to God in Christ Jesus", (Rom 6:11), "there is now no condemnation for those in Christ Jesus" (Rom 8:1), "we are all one body in Christ Jesus" (Rom 12:5), "Prisca and Aquila, my fellow workers in Christ Jesus" (Rom 16:3), "those sanctified in Christ Jesus" (1 Cor 1:2), "from him you are in Christ Jesus" (1 Cor 1:30) and "those who have fallen asleep in Christ" (1 Cor 15:18).[1] The phrase "in Christ" is synonymous with the term "in the Spirit". Paul tells us "…anyone who is joined to the Lord is one spirit with him" (1 Cor 6:17). Jesus calls us into communion with him. He enables us to call God "Abba, Father" (see Rom 8:15 and Gal 4:6). We are called to share in the same love that Jesus experienced. We are called to be one with him and know we are loved. We are beloved of God. As God delighted in his son the beloved (Mt 3:17) so he delights in us. We are God's beloved in the beloved. We come to experience we are loved and called to share in Jesus' prayer, life and love. This is why we can pray the "Our Father". (see Lk 11:1 and Mt 6:9).

Jesus' Prayer for his disciples:

In the Gospel of John (chapter 17) Jesus is coming near his death, the time of his "glorification". Now he turns to pray for his disciples. Jesus is now with the Father and in the Father. He raises his eyes to Heaven. This comes after Jesus had knelt and washed the feet of his disciples. Now he turns to God. Jesus says:

---

[1] see J.D.G. Dunn, The Theology of Paul the Apostle (Edinburgh: 2006).

'Father, the hour has come:
glorify your Son
so that your Son may glorify you;
and, through the power over all mankind that you have given him,
let him give eternal life to all those you have entrusted to him.
And eternal life is this:
to know you,
the only true God,
and Jesus Christ whom you have sent.'

(Jn 17:1-3)

When John uses the word "know" it means to have an experience of love. We are the ones Jesus leaves and he prays we share in the love between him and the Father. The Father is the source of life and love. Everything Jesus says and does comes from the Father. Jesus is the one sent to reveal the Father.

'I have glorified you on earth
and finished the work
that you gave me to do.
Now, Father, it is time for you to glorify me
with that glory I had with you
before ever the world was.
I have made your name known
to the men you took from the world to give me.
They were yours and you gave them to me,
and they have kept your word.
Now at last they know
that all you have given me comes indeed from you;
for I have given them
the teaching you gave to me,
and they have truly accepted this, that I came from you,
and have believed that it was you who sent me.'

(Jn 17:4-8)

Jesus is leading his friends into the glory of the life of God. In this he is glorified. He achieves this union by his death. He took into himself all alienation, all hostility and this led to his death. But God raised him from the dead. Love proved stronger than death (see Song 8:6). We are Jesus' friends (Jn 15:15) and in his love we can be fruitful (Jn 15:8). Irenaeus of Lyons (+202) said: "the glory of God is the human being fully alive". We are "alive" when we know the love of God. Having affirmed and confirmed his friends, Jesus prays for them:

> 'I pray for them;
> I am not praying for the world
> but for those you have given me,
> because they belong to you:
> all I have is yours
> and all you have is mine,
> and in them I am glorified.
> I am not in the world any longer,
> but they are in the world,
> and I am coming to you.
> Holy Father,
> keep those you have given me true to your name.
> I have watched over them and not one is lost
> except the one who chose to be lost,
> and this was to fulfill the scriptures.
> But now I am coming to you
> and while still in the world I say these things
> to share my joy with them to the full.
> I passed your word on to them,
> and the world hated them,
> because they belong to the world
> no more than I belong to the world.
> I am not asking you to remove them from the world,,
> but to protect them from the evil one.
> They do not belong to the world
> any more than I belong to the world.'

(Jn 17:8-19)

Jesus prays for those who continue his mission to reveal the Father and to share the gift of the Spirit. Human beings are a mixture of the presence of God and the absence of God. By ourselves we cannot bridge the gap that separates the infinite from the finite. God reaches out to us and welcomes us into his love. We grow as we leave behind (often very slowly) the worlds of darkness and selfishness in us, and open our hearts to compassionate love. We begin to know and love others as we are known and loved. We begin to welcome others as God knows and welcomes them. Jesus prays here that we would be one in God and one with each other. The Essene community which existed around the time of John speak of "their being gathered into the unity" (1QS 5:7). For John the "unity" into which we are called is the unity between the Father and Jesus. The disciples here heard "the word of God" from the word made flesh (Jn 1:14) and now are not part of the old world in which they grew up. The mission of Jesus was to witness to what he knew and experienced from the Father (Jn 3:32, 8:26). The disciples are called into union with Jesus and the Father and in this way they are cleansed. In John 17:21 and 23 Jesus speaks of the Father in him and he in the Father and then he speaks of the Father and the Son indwelling the believer by the power of the Holy Spirit. We come to know God by experiencing God's love for us revealed in Jesus (see Jn 14:23).

At the end of the prayer for his disciples, Jesus says:

'I want those you have given me
to be with me where I am,
so that they may always see the glory
you have given me
because you loved me
before the foundation of the world.
Father, Righteous One,
the world has not known you,
but I have known you,
and these have known
that you sent me.
I have made your name known to them
and will continue to make it known,

so that the love with which you loved me may be in them, and so that I may be in them.'

(Jn 17:24-27)

Jesus is the one who has brought us into community with God by the power of the Spirit (Jn 10:38, 14:10f, 14:23, 15:4-5). The glory is the human being fully alive in the love of God. The relationship between Jesus and the Father is one of love. The Spirit is the love between the Father and Jesus. Here the disciples are called to a deepening of their love for one another. We are called to love one another as Jesus has loved us (see Jn 13:34). Jesus showed us the depths of his love by submitting in love to the violence of this world and showing by his resurrection that this love overcomes all, even death. Jesus said "There is no greater love than to lay down one's life for one's friends" (Jn 15:13). This love is for us. The friends of Jesus are called to become one with Jesus in love by the power of the Holy Spirit and to become one with each other. This text was very close to St. Francis. In the 1st letter to all the Faithful he quotes this text. He delights in the figure of Jesus who is with us and prays for us.[2] Indeed for Francis the entire Gospel of John led us deep into a meeting with Jesus the Christ. We see this in his first admonition, where he quotes freely Jn 14:6:

'The Lord Jesus says to his disciples: I am the way, the truth and the life; no one comes to the Father except through me. If you knew me, you would also know my Father; and from now on, you do know him and have seen him. Philip says to him: Lord, show us the Father and it will be enough for us. Jesus says to him: Have I been with you for so long a time and you have not known me? Philip, whoever sees me sees my Father as well.
The Father dwells in inaccessible light, and God is spirit, and no one has ever seen God. Therefore He cannot be seen except in the Spirit because it is the Spirit that gives life; the

---

[2] see Regis Armstrong, J.A. Wayne Hellmen, William J. Short, Francis of Assisi - The Saint: Early Documents, Vol. 1 (New York: 1991) p. 41f, see also read Letter to all the Faithful and Earlier Rule, chapter 22 (p. 43f and 79f).

flesh has nothing to offer. But because He is equal to the Father, the Son is not seen by anyone other than the Father or other than the Holy Spirit.

All those who saw the Lord Jesus according to the humanity, therefore, and did not see and believe according to the Spirit and the Divinity that He is the true Son of God were condemned. Now in the same way, all those who see the sacrament sanctified by the words of the Lord upon the altar at the hands of the priest in the form of bread and wine, and who do not see and believe according to the Spirit and the Divinity that it is truly the Body and Blood of our Lord Jesus Christ, are condemned.'

(Admonition 1, ibid, p. 128)

Jesus in Gethsemane:

As Jesus' arrest, trial and death approach he finds himself in Gethsemane and we find ourselves with Jesus who has fallen to the ground (Mk 14:35). Jesus falls to the earth and experiences the testing, peirasmos. He feels a deep anxiety within, [Greek word *ekthambeisthai*] and the horror which isolates, [Greek word *ademonein*] (see Mk 14:33). This is a supreme loneliness where he feels an infinite distance between him and the Father. He pleads to his father when he calls 'Abba'. Yet there is silence. In agony he says yes to the will of the Father "Be it as you, not I, would have it" (Mk 14:36). Jesus is now utterly alone; those he asked to be with him, Peter, James and John, slept. They are unaware of what is to come and when Jesus is arrested they flee. Jesus, however, is ready because he prayed and became strong in his agony. Mark says in his Gospel:

They came to a small estate called Gethsemane, and Jesus said to his disciples, 'Stay here while I pray'. Then he took Peter and James and John with him. And a sudden fear came over him, and great distress. And he said to them, 'My soul is sorrowful to the point of death. Wait here, and keep awake.' And going on a little further he threw himself on the ground and prayed that, if it were possible, this hour might pass him by. 'Abba (Father)!' he said 'Everything is possible for you. Take this cup away from me. But let it be as you, not I would have it.' He came back and found them sleeping, and he said to Peter, 'Simon, are you asleep? Had you not the strength to keep awake for one hour? You should be awake, and praying not to be put to the test. The spirit is willing, but the flesh is weak.' Again he went away and prayed, saying the same words. And once more he came back and found them sleeping, their eyes were so heavy; and they could find no answer for him. He came back a third time and said to them

> 'You can sleep on now and take your rest. It is all over. The
> hour has come. Now the Son of Man is to be betrayed into
> the hands of sinners. Get up! Let us go! My betrayer is close
> at hand already.'

(Mk 14:32-42)

In Mark's version (see above) Jesus is presented as the obedient son of God who struggles to accept God's will in his passion. It presents the disciples as hopelessly unaware as he struggles. The name 'Gethsemane' means "oil press" and is found outside the east wall of Jerusalem. We see Jesus overcome by terror and fear (ademonein and ekthambeisthai). Jesus' soul is sorrowful unto death. Jesus goes back to the disciples who are with him. He urges them to wake and pray lest they fall into temptation. This is a teaching parallel to the teaching given to the disciples in the Lord's prayer (see Mt 6:9-13; Lk 11:2-4). The cup Jesus refers to is the cup of suffering. This expression has eucharistic connotations. Jesus abandons himself into God's hands accepting the cup of suffering. He says it should be as God wills. The idea of the temptation and trial (the peirasmos) that is coming refers to the trial that precedes the coming of God's kingdom (see Mk 13:9-13). Now that the 'hour has come' Jesus gathers himself and after his tears of agony is now ready. He says to the disciples: "You can sleep now and take your rest. It is all over. The hour has come. Now the Son of Man is to be betrayed into the hands of sinners. Get up! Let us go! My betrayer is close at hand already" (Mk 14:41f). The disciples because they have not prayed are not ready and when the hour comes they run away. Peter denies he knew Jesus (Mk 14:66-72).

The Lord's Prayer

The Lord's Prayer (also called the Our Father or Pater Noster, among other names) is a venerated Christian prayer that, according to the New Testament, Jesus taught as the way to pray. Two versions of this prayer are recorded: the long form in the Gospel of Matthew in the middle of the Sermon on the Mount, and the short form in the Gospel of Luke when "one of his disciples said to him, 'Lord, teach us to pray, as John taught his disciples.'"

The first three of the seven petitions in Matthew address God; the other four are related to human needs and concerns. The Matthew account alone includes the "Your will be done" and the "Rescue us from the evil one" (or "Deliver us from evil") petitions. Both original Greek texts contain the adjective epiousios, which does not appear in any other classical or Koine Greek literature; while controversial, "daily" has been the most common English-language translation of this word. Some Christians, particularly Protestants, conclude the prayer with a doxology, a later addendum appearing in some manuscripts of Matthew.

Matthew 6:9-13:
Our Father in heaven, hallowed be your name. Your kingdom come. Your will be done, on earth as it is in heaven. Give us this day our daily bread. And forgive us our debts, as we also have forgiven our debtors. And do not bring us to the time of trial, but rescue us from the evil one.

Luke 11:2-4:
Father, hallowed be your name. Your kingdom come. Give us each day our daily bread. And forgive us our sins, for we ourselves forgive everyone indebted to us. And do not bring us to the time of trial.

Initial words on the topic from the Catechism of the Catholic Church teach that it "is truly the summary of the whole gospel" (CCC, 2761). The prayer is used by most Christian churches in their worship; with few exceptions, the liturgical form is the Matthean. The "Our Father" in Matthew is similar to the 18 Benedictions and the Qaddish prayer of the synagogue. It addresses God as Father and asks forgiveness. The kingdom means the will of God on earth and we are taught to pray that God's will may be done on earth. "Our Father in Heaven" is the new way of addressing the one who was called Yahweh in the Old Testament. "Thy kingdom come" refers to the peace, love and joy of the Holy Spirit (see Rom 14:17). "Our daily bread" refers to our prayer that God look over us. The Greek word "epiousion", translated as daily, is a difficult word to translate. It can mean the bread we need or the bread for the future. In the end we trust in God to provide for us. We pray that our debts (our sins) be forgiven and in experiencing forgiveness we extend this forgiveness to others. God is more merciful and generous than we are (see Matt 18:21-35; 20:1-16). We are called to follow his lead in forgiveness. The final "lead us not" probably means do not let us succumb in the final trial, but keep us safe in his care and providence. Tertullian (+240 AD) called the Lord's prayer "the summary of the whole gospel" and the Catechism of the Catholic Church follows him in this.

Prayer involves us speaking to God. He is "Our Father in Heaven". When we pray the "Our Father" we are in communion with all our brothers and sisters who pray these words. He is different from us but we are called into a relationship with him. He is personal. We trust him to give good things to his children (Matt 7:11). We pray that God's name be held holy. According to Ezekiel 36:23-33, God would make his name holy by gathering people together, cleansing them from sin and giving them a new spirit. We become fully human when we know God's love and forgiveness and are vivified by his life-giving Spirit.

St. Teresa of Avila:

Teresa was able to communicate her experience in prayer. Experiencing is not a sensation of something ("I experienced pain when I touched the fire"), but it means becoming experienced in something by having engaged with it. One could speak of someone who was a wine-taster. Experience is a dynamic and relational term. Throughout her works Teresa speaks about what she experienced when she prayed. As Gillian Ahlgren put it, "One of her unique gifts as a theologian is her ability to create and shape a narrative interpretation of personal experience that reveals to the readers the reality of God who is active in human affairs and engages us to see the presence of God in our own life journeys."[3] Teresa described the mystical graces she received. In one part of her Spiritual Testimonies she said, her prayer is not intellectual in a discursive way (i.e. meditation) but is "a recollection and elevation of spirit that comes upon me so suddenly I cannot resist" (Spiritual Testimonies, 1.2). A second type is described by Teresa as a "very intense, consuming impulse for God I cannot resist", which involves pain "as well as a certain rapture in which everything is made peaceful" (Spiritual Testimonies, 1.3). A third grace she received is apostolic: "At other times some desire to serve God came upon me with impulses so strong that I don't know how to exaggerate them" (1.4). She summarises these mystical graces: "All those desires and these, too, for virtue were given to me by our Lord after he gave me the prayer of quiet with these raptures and I found I was so improved that it seems to me I previously was a total loss" (1.8). The background to Teresa's life was complex. She was a woman in a male-dominated world and there was the constant background of the Inquisition. As Deirdre Green put it: "Teresa was working within an oppressive, racist, sexist and fanatically dogmatic system" and in spite of "her vulnerability as a woman, a converso [i.e. of Jewish background] and a visionary, she managed to escape serious condemnation".[4] It was from this background Teresa forged her prayer life.

Saint Teresa of Avila, baptised as Teresa Sanchez de Cepeda y Ahumada (1515-1582), was a reformer of the Carmelite order and she was an important writer on prayer. The disciples asked Jesus to teach them to pray. He taught them the Our Father (see Mt 6:9-13) and he also tells them to go into their room and pray to the Father in secret (Mt 6:5-9). Teresa lived out Jesus' teaching and when she wrote she described how she prayed (Life, Introduction 1) drawing others into the life of prayer.

She meditated on the scene in the Garden of Gethsemane and one day she saw a representation of Jesus praying in Gethsemane. She was deeply moved by what she saw. She saw Jesus alone and in need of love.

---

[3] G. Ahlgren, Entering Teresa of Avila's Castle: A Reader's Companion (Minneapolis: 2016) p. 9.

[4] Deirdre Green, Gold in the Crucible: Teresa of Avila and the Western Mystical Tradition (Shaftesbury: 1989) p. 145f.

She desired to relieve his agony. This drew her deeper into prayer as she continued to ponder Jesus. She had begun to practice real prayer (Life, IX,4). Jesus was real for her and now in prayer she knew he was alive and close to her. She had a sense even as a child of the love of God and she and her brother Rodrigo spoke of being martyred for love of Jesus. Her parents intervened (Life, I,4). Now years later she rediscovered her fervour. She still had to fight many distractions but through it all she began to grow in love (Life, X,5).

When she entered the convent of the Visitation she was drawn into the worldly life of the convent and for many years she was lukewarm in her prayer-life. She points out that God is always close to us, but we are unaware of his presence because we are caught up in many things. However when we begin to practice prayer we become aware of his presence by the power of the Holy Spirit (see Life VIII,2). Before Teresa reached this state of prayer she tells us she had to battle with the "world" and friendship with God, but in the end friendship with God won out.

"I suffered this battle and conflict between friendship with God and friendship with the world. During the remaining years of which I have yet to speak, the cause of the war changed, although the war was not a small one. But since it was, in my opinion, for the service of God and with knowledge of the vanity that the world is, everything went smoothly as I shall say afterward.

I have recounted all this at length, as I already mentioned, so that the mercy of God and my ingratitude might be seen; also, in order that one might understand the great good God does for a soul that willingly disposes itself for the practice of prayer, even though it is not disposed as is necessary. I recount this also that one may understand how if the soul perseveres in prayer, in the midst of the sins, temptations and failures of a thousand kinds that the devil places in its path, in the end, I hold as certain, the Lord will draw it forth to the harbor of salvation as now it seems He did for me. May it please His Majesty that I do not get lost again."

(Life, VIII,3-4)

Her aim is to invite us to share this same friendship. God is always present to us and he loves and accepts us. It is we who drift from him but Teresa teaches us to pick ourselves up and draw closer to the one who is always present to us. It was the figure of the lonely Jesus in Gethsemane that re-awoke Teresa's life with God. His agony shows us the depth of his love. He was prepared to endure this, so that we might have life. By the power of the Holy Spirit Jesus is alive to us today. The agony of so many people is the agony of Jesus. When we can be with him we share his prayer for suffering humanity. Pascal said: "Jesus will be in agony until the end of the world, we must not sleep during this time" (Pensées, Penguin Books, 1966, p. 313). Jesus is present in the heart of all who suffer. Teresa tells us Jesus will never force us to come to him. He awaits our response (Life VIII,9). Coming to know Jesus and his mercy is something we must work on and await God's grace. Teresa describes her battle in the following words:

"When I was with God, my attachments to the world disturbed me. This is a war so troublesome that I don't know how I was able to suffer it even a month, much less for so many years.

However, I see clearly the great mercy the Lord bestowed on me; for though I continued to associate with the world, I had the courage to practice prayer. I say courage, for I do not know what would require greater courage among all the things there are in the world than to betray the king and know that he knows it and yet never leave His presence. Though we are always in the presence of God, it seems to me the manner is different with those who practice prayer, for they are aware that He is looking at them. With others, it can happen that several days pass without their even once recollecting that God sees them."

(Life VIII,2)

She described prayer as friendship with God and she was drawn into this friendship. Prayer is friendship with God who always loves us.

As we saw Teresa turned again to dedicate herself to prayer when she beheld an image of the suffering Jesus in Gethsemane. Here are her own words to describe her coming back to friendship with God.

"But in this latter instance with this statue I am speaking of, it seems to me I profited more, for I was very distrustful of myself and placed all my trust in God. I think I then said that I would not rise from there until He granted what I was begging Him for. I believe certainly this was beneficial to me, because from that time I went on improving.

This is the method of prayer I then used: since I could not reflect discursively with the intellect, I strove to picture Christ within me, and it did me greater good – in my opinion – to picture Him in those scenes where I saw Him more alone. It seemed to me that being alone and afflicted, as a person in need, He had to accept me. I had many simple thoughts like these. The scene of His prayer in the garden, especially, was a comfort to me; I strove to be His companion there. If I could, I thought of the sweat and agony He had undergone in that place. I desired to wipe away the sweat He so painfully experienced, but I recall that I never dared to actually do it, since my sins appeared to me so serious. I remained with Him as long as my thoughts allowed me to, for there were many distractions that tormented me. Most nights, for many years before going to bed, when I commended myself to God in preparation for sleep, I always pondered for a little while this episode of the prayer in the garden. I did this even before I was a nun since I was told that one gains many indulgences by doing so. I believe my soul gained a great deal..."

(Life IX,3-4)

Teresa, in all her major works, The Life, The Way of Perfection, The Interior Castle, explains the practice of prayer. In her autobiography she uses the image of water to illustrate our advancing in prayer. The first way to draw water is to use a bucket and a rope. Using these we can draw water from the well. In prayer this is an image Teresa uses to speak of vocal prayer and discursive meditation. This is an active method of prayer. Beginners can think too much so Teresa advises "…let them imagine themselves in the presence of Christ, and let them continue conversing with him and delighting in him, without wearying their minds or exhausting themselves by composing speeches to him (Life, XIII,11).

The next method of watering the garden is by irrigation using the water of a running stream. In prayer this means having all our faculties centered on God. It does not involve the work used in the first method. Teresa calls it a "sleep of the faculties" because they rest in God. "Not one of them, it seems, ventures to stir, nor can we cause any of them to be active except by striving to fix our attention very carefully on something else, and even then I don't think we could succeed in doing so" (Life, XVI,3). This is the prayer of quiet and is a "union of the entire soul with God" (Life XVII,3).

The next image Teresa uses is that of the falling rain on the garden. This is where prayer is infused into the heart by the power of the Holy Spirit. We are now in union with God. Teresa recalls her desiring of this union when she reflected on the meeting of the Samaritan Woman and Jesus (Jn 4:4-26). Jesus tells the woman "… whoever drinks the water that I will give them will never thirst. Indeed the water I will give them will become in them a spring of water welling up to eternal life" (Jn 4:14). This is the life of the Spirit and a life of union with Jesus in the Spirit. This is what Teresa calls the prayer of union. She describes her longing for this union:

> These impulses are like some little springs I've seen flowing, they never cease to move the sand upward. This is a good example of, or comparison to, souls that reach this state: love is always stirring and thinking; about what it will do. It cannot contain itself, just as that water doesn't seem to fit in the earth; but the earth casts it out of itself. So is the soul very habitually, for by reason of the love it has it doesn't rest in or contain itself. It is already soaked in this

water, it would want others to drink, since it has no lack of water, so that they might help it praise God. Oh, how many times do I recall the living water that the Lord told the Samaritan woman about! And so I am very fond of that gospel passage. Thus it is, indeed, that from the time I was a little child, without understanding this good as I do now, I often begged the Lord to give me the water. I always carried with me a painting of this episode of the Lord at the well, with the words, inscribed Domine, da mihi aquam.

(Life XXX,19)

St. Augustine's 'Confessions' also played a part in Teresa's development. Seeing the figure of Jesus suffering and the reading of the "Confessions' set her firmly on a life of prayer. She says:

Considering the love He bore me, I regained my courage, for I never lost confidence in His mercy, in myself, I lost it many times.

Oh, God help me, how it frightens me, my soul's blindness despite so much assistance from God! It made me fearful to see how little I could do by myself and how bound I became so that I was unable to resolve to give myself entirely to God.

As I began to read the Confessions, it seemed to me I saw myself in them. I began to commend myself very much to this glorious saint. When I came to the passage where he speaks about his conversion and read how he heard that voice in the garden, it only seemed to me, according to what I felt in my heart, that it was I the Lord called. I remained for a long time totally dissolved in tears and feeling within myself utter distress and weariness. Oh, how a soul suffers, God help me, by losing the freedom it should have in being itself; and what torments it undergoes! I marvel now at how I could have lived in such great affliction. May God be praised who gave me the life to rise up from a death so deadly.

(Life IX,8)

She now overcame her struggle between the divine intimacy with God and her independent selfhood, because now her selfishness was diminished and she was more attentive to God and to other people. The hallmark of her life after this was an ever increasing generativity. She initiated and carried out the reform of Carmel, founding over a dozen reformed convents throughout Spain and she became a prolific spiritual writer. Through her writing of the 'Life' she could see a pattern, a coherence in the way she was led to union with God. There has been interest in the last few years in the 'theology of story'. This has enriched our view of Teresa as both a storylistener and storyteller. Her message is carried by the story she tells.

A Storylistener

St. Peter of Alcantara, O.F.M. (1499-1562) was a Franciscan Friar. He met Teresa and saw in her a chosen one of God and her success in the reform of Carmel owes a lot to Peter's encouragement. Teresa suffered from a bout of anxiety but Peter soothed her spirit and she found peace in his counsel and direction. There was a friend of Teresa's, a widow, who arranged for Teresa to meet Peter (Life XXX,1-3). He took great pity on Teresa and was kind to her. He also helped those who were concerned about Teresa and didn't quite understand the effects God was working in her soul (Life XXX,6). She then tells us:

> We agreed that from then on I would write to him about what happened to me and that we would pray a good deal for each other. For such was his humility that he esteemed the prayers of this miserable one – which brought much embarrassment to me. He left me with the greatest consolation and happiness and the ability to feel secure in my prayer and not doubt that it was from God; he told me that if I had some doubt about anything, I should make it known to my confessor, and that in this way I would live safely.
> But I wasn't able to feel this assurance completely, because the Lord led me by the way of fear, in which I believed an experience was from the devil when they told me it was.

Thus no-one could make me so feel either fear or assurance that I could give my experiences more credence than that which the Lord placed in my soul. Hence even though Friar consoled and calmed me, I didn't give his words such credence as to be totally without fear, especially when the Lord left me in the trials of soul of which I shall now speak. Nevertheless, I remained, as I say, very consoled. I couldn't give enough thanks to God and to my glorious father St. Joseph, for it seemed to me that since Friar Peter was the general of the commissariat, it was St. Joseph who brought him here; for the commissariat is under the guardianship of St. Joseph, – to whom I prayed very much, as I did also to our Lady.

(Life, XXX,7)

Teresa had begun to receive mystical favours and some people had believed they were diabolical. This is the reason for Teresa's anxiety. Peter told her to praise God and what was taking place in her heart was the work of the Holy Spirit. Teresa met Peter about the year 1560 and he helped give outward expression to her inner experience of prayer. Peter's story became part of Teresa's and by listening to his story and experience she was released to pray deeply. She had a sense of the physical (though invisible) presence of Christ. She could begin to say with St. Paul: "I have been crucified with Christ; it is no longer I who live but Christ lives in me, and the life which I now live in the flesh I live by faith in the Son of God, who loved me and gave himself for me" (Gal 2:20).

Teresa was reared in a close-knit family of readers. She was an avid reader from childhood and she love books: her writings tell us of the books she read. She read contemporary fiction when she was young. Later she read the Fathers of the Church, St. Jerome's Epistle, St. Augustine's 'Confessions' and St. Gregory the Great's commentary on the Book of Job, and the 'Imitation of Christ'.

One particular author who helped shape her vision was Francisco de Osuna (+1541). His work 'The Third Spiritual Alphabet' greatly influenced St. Teresa (see Life IV,7). Francisco was a Franciscan friar. Another friar whose writings influenced Teresa was Bernardino de Laredo (+1540). His work 'The Ascent of Mount Sion' was useful for Teresa (Life XXIII,12). Teresa read what they had to say and used their thought selectively. She learned to recollect herself using Osuna and the stilling of thoughts she learned from Bernardino. Recollection and the prayer of quiet affect the higher part of the should allowing it to reach eternal realities.[5] This stillness leads us deep into our hearts. It leads us to our innermost being, where we can experience darkness. However the Spirit of God comes upon us and says "Let there be Light" (Abécédaire, p. 380). This is a reference to Genesis where we read: "In the beginning God created the heavens and the earth. Now the earth was formless and empty, darkness was over the surface of the deep, and the Spirit of God was hovering over the waters. And God said 'Let there be light' and there was light" (Gen 1:1-3). Creation is ongoing and in quietness and trust the Spirit can bring light out of our darkness. Love heals and transforms. St. Paul puts it this way: "If anyone is in Christ, the new creation has come. The old has gone, the new is here" (2 Cor 5:17). We find God lives in our innermost being. In John 14:23 we read "Anyone who loves me will obey my teaching. My Father will love them and we will come to them and make our home with them" and "The one who loves me [Jesus] will be loved by my Father, and I too will love them and show myself to them" (Jn 14:21).

It was in Bernardino she learned to quiet her mind and her thoughts. He taught Teresa to wait in silence. Before we placeourselves before God we have to be still. Bernardino says "When I possess God alone, I possess in him all things that it is possible to possess; if with God I owned all creation, I would not be as rich as I would be possessing God alone"[6] Thus when the soul is occupied with the things of God it need not concern itself with other things. Teresa speaks of the prayer of recollection in the Interior Castle (IC, IV,3.3). Teresa speaks of finding Jesus in her heart (Life IV,7) and she would later write about a loving

---

[5] see Francisco de Osuna, Troisieme abécédaire (Madrid: 1911), p. 399 (Abécédaire in text).

[6] see Fidèle de Ros, Le Frère Bernardin de Laredo (Paris: 1948), p. 325-326. He quotes from Monte Sion, 1538, III, c.27.

conversation with Jesus. She would speak of a heart to heart conversation:

> "O Lord of the world, my true spouse (You can say this to him if he has moved your heart to pity at seeing him thus, for not only will you desire to look at him but you will also delight in speaking with him, not with readymade prayers but with those that come from the sorrow of your heart..."
>
> (The Way of Perfection, 26.6)

Teresa remained close to the humanity of Christ. In the passage quoted above she once again meditated on Jesus suffering who asked for friends to be with him to console him (Way of Perfection, 26.2). Her emphasis on the humanity of Christ is her own and in this she differed from Bernardino. She says:

> "In thinking about and carefully examining what the Lord suffered for us, we are moved to compassion; and this sorrow and the resulting tears bring delight. In thinking about the glory we hope for, the love that God bore for us, and his resurrection we are moved to a joy that is neither entirely spiritual nor entirely of the senses. But the joy is virtuous..."
>
> (Life XII,1)

We must allow ourselves welcome the presence of Jesus to us. This is where the prayer of quiet comes in. Prayer is the cultivation of this friendship with Jesus. She says: "What more could we desire from such a good friend at our side? Unlike our friends in the world, he will never abandon us when we are troubled or distressed. Blessed is the one who truly loves him and always keeps him near" (Life XXII,6) and "Whenever we think of Christ, we should recall the love that led him to bestow on us so many graces and favours, and also the great love God showed us in giving us in Christ a pledge of his love" (Life XXII,7). Teresa listened to others but was able to make her own synthesis. She listened to the story of others but she was able to make her own story from the stories of others.

The Interior Castle:

When we think of Teresa we must remember she lived in the time of the Spanish Inquisition. This was established by the Catholic monarchs Ferdinand II of Aragon (+1516) and Isabella I of Castille (+1504). Teresa had to be careful what she said so as not to fall foul of the Inquisition. She had been ordered to write her autobiography "La Vida de la Santa Madre Teresa de Jesús (The Life of the Holy Mother Teresa of Jesús). She did begin work on interior prayer in a work which became known as "The Interior Castle". She started writing on June 2, 1577, Trinity Sunday, and finished on St. Andrew's Day, 29 November, 1578. She was aware that her autobiography was in the hands of the Inquisition. This was not the best of times for writing on Interior prayer. Under this pressure she still produced one of the masterpieces of Spanish literature. The years 1575-1577 saw a great increase in tensions between the Carmelite friars over Teresa's reforms and with John of the Cross (+1591) who worked with Teresa. In 1577 John was kidnapped and was left without protection. The Papal Nuncio who had protected him had died. This was a turbulent time for Teresa. Our faith may be in turmoil and our life in tumult. Teresa tells us that then we should pray. We must flee towards God. In the first pages of the 'Castle' she describes the 'beautiful and delightful Castle' that is the soul. God himself has chosen to dwell in the soul. He is the sun who gives all the splendour and beauty that is the soul's, by living at the centre of the soul. This presence of God in the soul is accomplished by the Holy Spirit. Paul speaks of the believer being a temple of the Holy Spirit (see 1 Cor 3:17; 1 Cor 6:19-20; 2 Cor 6:16) and John speaks of the soul as the place where God dwells (Jn 14:23). In the centre of the soul "all three persons communicate themselves to it [the soul], speak to it and explain these words of the Lord in the Gospel: that he and the Father and the Holy Spirit will come to dwell with the soul that loves him and keeps his commandments" (Castle, 7,1.6). It is by the inspiration of the Holy Spirit through Christ that we come to the Father (cf Rom 8:14-17; Gal 4:4-7 and Eph 1:3-14). She describes the soul in the following way:

> "...a most beautiful crystal globe, made in the shape of a castle, and containing seven mansions, in the seventh and

innermost of which was the King of Glory, in the greatest splendour, illumining and beautifying them all. The nearer one got to the centre, the stronger was the light; outside the palace limits everything was foul, dark and infested with toads, vipers and other venomous creatures."

(Castle 1,1.1)

She speaks of the great reality that fills the soul, the sun that shines in it and the fountain of life that springs up within it. With infectious enthusiasm she speaks of the splendour of the soul, the dignity of the person. She speaks of how we darken our dignity by sin. We lose sight of the sun "who has given it all splendour and beauty, and is still there at the centre of the soul" (Castle 1,1.2). The door to the entrance of the castle is prayer and reflection (ibid. 1,1.7). For Teresa it is important for us to know that the soul is a 'Paradise' for God in which he takes his delight (Castle1,1.1). To know God and the riches he pours out into the soul is for Teresa the first knowledge to be acquired and we come to know ourselves in God. We discover we are deeply loved and of infinite value. Coming close to God in prayer we overcome alienation from ourselves, from others and from God. Our journey begins with self-knowledge, and prayer and meditation. We know ourselves in God and the dignity he has called us to.

"Even when we are engaged in our worldly pastimes and businesses and pleasures and hagglings, when we are falling into sins and rising from them again ... in spite of all that, this Lord of ours is so anxious that we should desire Him and strive after His companionship that He calls us ceaselessly, time after time, to approach Him ... and the poor soul is consumed with grief at being unable to do His bidding immediately."

(Castle 2,1.2)

Teresa wrote for her sisters in Carmel, but her fame has spread far beyond the cloister walls. In the next few chapters, or rooms of the Castle, she speaks about organising our lives to find God who lives at the centre of the soul. The person living in the world can still find her advice useful and make plans in his or her world to pray. All our lives, our asceticism is subordinated to our quest for God. Perfection for her is being united with God. Teresa says there is no evil as great as that of not being at ease in our own house. "What hope can we have of finding rest outside ourselves if we cannot be at rest within?" (Castle, 2,1.9). It is only when we are loved truly and infinitely can we be at home with ourselves. This is the journey Teresa takes us on. She encourages the soul to seek every opportunity for growth, by listening to sermons, and in partaking of good conversation.

The third mansion is that of a good life. Here the soul comes to know itself and its weakness. It sees the danger of trusting in its own strength. We can understand the third mansion as a space of greater mindfulness, and personal integration. Teresa says some people here might presume God's goodness or they might think of relationship with God as a sort of transaction, "if I abide by God's law, I will get rewarded". This stage "represents either a point of entry into deeper transformative relationship with God or the end of the road for those who equate religion with its codes, creeds and rituals."[7] In John of the Cross' writings this stage parallels what John said: "desiring, for the sake of Christ, to enter into poverty, emptiness and self stripping with respect to all that is in the world" (Ascent of Mount Carmel, 1:13).

John was ordained a priest in 1567 and for a while he thought of joining the Carthusian order with emphasised solitary and silent contemplation. Around 1567 he met Teresa. She talked to him about how she was seeking to reform the Carmelite order. Teresa asked John to delay his entry into the Carthusians and follow her. John agreed and in November 1568 John and a companion were given the use of a derelict house at Duruelo. He took the name John of the Cross. He came to influence Teresa and his influence can be seen in Teresa's mature writings. Teresa and John said if we were to love truly we should go directly to the source and loving teacher of all love. The painful truth of our reality is that the frustrations of daily life, our own personal weaknesses and darkness, and the pain of being human often keep us from feeling and

---

[7] Gillian T. W. Ahlgren, Entering Teresa of Avila's Interior Castle (Minneapolis: 2016) p. 39.

expressing the love that we might be capable of. John and Teresa tell us that to love is to be in a constant process of purification and refinement. The method John and Teresa teach is contemplative prayer, that takes place in silence, stillness and the interior of a person. That is the journey Teresa leads us on in the Interior Castle. In the third mansion or room the soul has to endure a spirit of aridity, but this is not a backsliding but part of the process of transformation in love.

In the fourth mansion our world and the world of the Spirit meet. In this mansion the soul does not depend on its own efforts. Here we draw life from God. Love doesn't come from an aqueduct but flows from the source of all living water. It has left all that hinders it: Here the inner heart is enlarged and expanded as it experiences love. No further growth is possible unless the soul develops its capacity to love. We begin to realise, whatever our circumstances, we can bring a loving disposition to bear in every situation: "Perhaps we do know what love is ... it doesn't consist in great delight but in desiring with a strong determination to please God in everything..." (Castle IV,1:7).

Teresa shares her experience with prayer. Prayer is more about opening oneself to God's presence as one is, where one is. The signs of love are our desire to reach out in compassion. It is difficult to "erase" our minds when we sit in silence. She writes: "Ordinarily the mind flies about quickly; only God can hold it in such a way as to make it seem that we are somehow loosed from the body" (Castle IV,1.8). Teresa admits: "I have been very afflicted at times in the midst of the turmoil of the mind... it was an arduous thing for me that my intellect should be so restless at times (ibid, 1:8). John and Teresa showed a pastoral tenderness to those who struggle with the mind racing here, there and everywhere. She says: "We must let the mill-clapper keep clacking on, and must continue grinding our flour, not stopping our work with the will and the understanding" (Castle IV, 1;12f).We must remain in silence and prayerful meditation – God in his time will come. "In order to truly profit by this path and ascend to the dwelling places we desire, the important thing is not to think much but to love much; and so do that which best stirs love in you" (Castle, IV,1:7). When we accept ourselves in this state then gradually the "interior works are all gentle and peaceful... Leave the soul in God's hands; let God do what God will with it, with the greatest disinterest about your own benefit as is possible and the greatest turning over of the self into God" (Castle IV,3:6).

In the fifth mansion we begin to understand the particularity and depth of God's love for us. God becomes known in a more profound and intimate way as here the soul "comes to understand that God cherishes it, and has chosen it for union, in the same way that spouses choose and dedicate themselves to each other."[8] Now we come to know ourselves in the light of the love of God and we are enfolded in his great love. We come to live by the way God loves us and we bring that love to others. In his 'Life of the Beloved' Henri Nouwen tries to express what the term chosen by God to be his beloved means:

"From all eternity, long before you were born, you existed in God's heart. ...The eyes of love had seen you as precious, as of infinite beauty, as of eternal value. When love chooses, it chooses with a perfect sensitivity for the unique beauty of the chosen one; and it chooses without making anyone feel excluded."[9]

We are all God's chosen. The words of Teresa and Henri Nouwen lead us to see ourselves as the beloved of God. The power of the love of God transforms us. We come to be in union with God. "This union is above all earthly joys, above all delights, above all consolations, and still more than that..." (Castle V,1:5). Teresa uses the language of the spouses, drawing her images from the Song of Songs (Castle V,1:11).

In Luke 3:22 we read "...the Holy Spirit descended on him [Jesus] in bodily form like a dove. And a voice came from Heaven, 'You are my Son, my beloved, in whom I am well pleased'. Jesus by making peace with God has made us friends and children of God. We are his beloved in the Beloved. She uses the image of how the silkworm comes to be. We are reborn in Christ. Our whole life is Christ (Castle V,1:12). His majesty (Christ) places us in this union and he enters into the centre of

[8] G.T.W. Ahlgren, op. cit., p. 68.
[9] Henri J.M. Nouwen, Life of the Beloved (New York: 1992) p. 53f.

our soul. There the soul loves God and God loves the soul in return. We are like a silkworm who spins a cocoon to prepare for the day it becomes a moth or a butterfly, so the soul is to build a house through the prayer of union in preparation for the day when God will transform the soul into his likeness (Castle V,2:2-4). When we allow the silkworm die to be born again we come to live in union with God. We sometimes experience deeply this love "…it is short in duration, but while it lasts, the soul is completely possessed by God" (Castle V,1,9, Peers Translation, p. 62).

The sixth mansion is a preparation for the life of full union with God. We are being transformed into the Lover who loves us into new life. We begin to know God here as the supreme lover and the source of all love. We are also invited by God to share the love we experience into the world as we find it and where we find ourselves. In this mansion "the soul is now wounded with love for its spouse, and strives for more opportunities to be alone and, in conformity with its state, to rid itself of everything that can be an obstacle to this solitude" (Castle, VI,1:1). Teresa tells us that great misunderstandings and sufferings can come to the soul in this mansion. She speaks of the experience of going to a confessor who declares and condemns everything as being from the devil or melancholy (Castle VI,1;8). "There is no remedy in this tempest but to wait for the mercy of God. For at an unexpected time, with one word or a chance happening, God so quickly calms the storm that it seems there had not been even so much as a cloud in that soul, and it remains filled with sunlight and much more consolation" (Castle VI,1:10). She speaks of a soul that had to suffer years of ill health and other sufferings before entering this mansion (Castle VI,1:7). Here she was referring to herself.

Teresa goes on to describe the ways God awakens the soul to new life. She describes how the soul is wounded by love. "It feels that it is being wounded in the most exquisite way, but it doesn't know how or by whom it is wounded. It knows clearly that the wound is something precious, and it would never want to be cured …But the soul would never want to be deprived of this pain. The wound satisfies it more than the delightful and painless absorption of the prayer of quiet" (Castle

VI,2:2). The action of love on the soul is powerful in this stage. Teresa goes on to speak of mystical states of rapture and locutions and advises the soul how to react in these states.

However advanced we might think we are we should never lose sight of the humanity of Jesus Christ (Castle VI,7:5). The soul desires to be completely taken up in love. We might become conscious of our failures and weaknesses. This keeps us humble and grounded. We need forgiveness and acceptance, but here we learn to walk with Christ. Teresa uses the image of 'betrothal' for this mansion. It is like an engagement.

Spiritual marriage occurs in the seventh mansion – here the soul is united with God as bride and bridegroom are united in marriage. Here the full realisation of the journey to union with God is realised. We live a life in relationship with God as Father, Son and Holy Spirit. Christ has become a bridge for us to enter this life. Love flows from one person to another in the Trinity. We share in this flow of love. Jesus said "Anyone who loves me will obey my teaching. My Father will love them and we will come to them and make our home with them" (Jn 14:23). This indwelling is the work of the Holy Spirit. Teresa speaks of the experience of living what Jesus said here. Teresa says "...all three persons communicate themselves to it, speak to it and explain these words of the Lord in the Gospel: that He and the Father and the Holy Spirit will come to dwell with the soul that loves him and keeps his commandments. (Castle VII,1:6) Every day the soul becomes more amazed, for these persons never seem to leave it any more" (Castle VII,1:7). Teresa describes the union using another image: "let us say that the union is like the joining of two wax candles to the extent that the flame coming from them is one, or that the wick, the flame and the wax are all one" (Castle VII,2:4). She goes on to say: "Perhaps this is what St. Paul means in saying 'He who is joined or united to the Lord is one spirit with him' (1 Cor 6:17)" (Castle VIII,2:5). We are not completely without fear or sin even here, but the fear is much less and we are more sensitive to our faults and sin. Suffering might still form part of our life here. We think of St. Thérèse of Lisieux who suffered even though she lived a life of love in God. Jesus gives certain souls a share in his vocation as suffering servant. It is as if we are called to comfort God in his sufferings.[10] The souls still have an inner strength that comes from union with God. They don't seek consolation or spiritual delights, since the Lord himself is present with these souls (Castle VII,3:8). "The Cross is not wanting but it doesn't disquiet or make the souls, who live in union with God, lose peace" (Castle VII,3:15). Teresa sees the prayer of union as uniting the vocations of Martha and Mary. Martha was seen as a model for the active life and Mary for the contemplative life. When we live the life of love then it must take expression in our daily lives. There are always opportunities for love where we are. Thérèse would also have this insight. We are called to serve all in love. Christ has been Teresa's companion throughout her journey. In the beginning she says: "…we should set our eyes on Christ, our good and on his saints" (Castle I,11:12). At the end of the journey she says: "Fix your eyes on the Crucified and everything will become small for you" (Castle VII,4:8). He is the way, the truth and the life for us (Jn 14:6).

The Ecstasy of Saint Teresa:

The ecstasy of Saint Teresa is the central sculpture in the Cornaro Chapel in Santa Maria della Vittoria in Rome. It was designed by Gian Lorenzo Bernini (+1680), the leading sculptor of his day. The two central sculptural figures of the swooning nun and the angel with a spear come from an episode in the 'Life' of St. Teresa. She writes:

I saw in his hand a long spear of gold, and at the iron's point there seemed to be a little fire. He appeared to me to be thrusting it at times into my heart, and to pierce my very entrails; when he drew it out, he seemed to draw them out also, and to leave me all on fire with a great love of God. The pain was so great, that it made me moan; and yet so surpassing was the sweetness of this excessive pain, that I could not wish to be rid of it. The soul is satisfied now with nothing less than God. The pain is not bodily, but spiritual;

---

[10] see my 'With Thee Tender is the Night' (CreateSpace: 2016).

though the body has its share in it. It is a caressing of love so sweet which now takes place between the soul and God, that I pray God in His goodness to make him experience it who may think that I am lying.

(Life XXIX, 19)

The image brings to life the words spoken by Teresa.

Other witnesses appear on the side walls of the chapel. They are members of the Cornaro family who commissioned the work. They observe what is going on, they see Teresa as if she is lying on a cloud. This emphasises the other-wordly nature of Teresa's ecstasy. They can symbolise us who look at Teresa and her experiences. We come to see the divine in her life and ask ourselves can we too come to know God and know his love in our hearts?

Edith Stein (+1942) tells the story of her conversion. She had lost the faith of her youth and was always searching for truth. She picked up the autobiography of St. Teresa and read it all night. "When I had finished the book, I said to myself: This is the truth." Later looking back on her life she said: "My longing for truth was a single prayer".[11]

---

[11] see Pope John Paul II, Teresa Benedicta of the Cross Edith Stein (1891-1942), words used by John Paul on the canonisation of Edith Stein, 1 May 1987, in Cologne (Vatican.va).

Chapter 4

The Canticle of Canticles:

The title of this book 'Canticle of Canticles' or 'Song of Songs' is a Hebrew idiom for the superlative. It means the greatest song. Rabbi Akiba (+135) said: "All the books of the Bible are holy, but the Canticle is the holiest of all. The world itself is not worthy of the day the Canticle was written." Origen (+254) was a Greek scholar, ascetic and early Christian theologian, born in Alexandria. He praised the spirit of the person who would understand the message of the Canticle (PG 131:37). The Canticle had an allegorical interpretation both in the Synagogue and the early Christian Church. The Canticle was taken to refer to the love of God for his people, and, for the Christian, it was taken to refer to the love of Christ for the Church or for the individual soul. The view of marriage as allegory is supported by the reading of the Book of Hosea. He used the image of marriage between God and his people to teach how much God loved his people (Hos 1-3, see also Isa 62:5). Hosea says:

> "...she [Israel] will say 'I will go back to my first husband'. That is why I am going to love her and lead her out into the wilderness and speak to her heart."
>
> (Hosea 2:18f)

Jewish writers in the Targum[1] treated the song as an allegory of the history of Israel (See R.E. Murphy in CBQ 43 (1981), p. 505-16).

In its original form the Canticle is a collection of love poems. In the poetry, human sexual love is seen as good and part of God's creation.

---

[1] The targum (plural: targumim) were spoken paraphrases, explanations and expansions of the Jewish scriptures, that a rabbi would give in the common language of the listeners, which was often Aramaic. The targum came about as Aramaic replaced the older Hebrew. In this chapter the quotes come from: "The Targum of Canticles", translated by Philip S. Alexander, The Aramaic Bible (Collegeville: MN: 2003). See also: Song of Songs Rabbah, trans. Maurice Simon; Midrash Rabbah (London: 1930). Quotes from the Targum are taken from Robert W. Jenson, Interpretation: Song of Songs (Louisville: 2005).

The commentators saw human love was seen as a symbol of divine love. The original song was a celebration of love between the bride and bridegroom and a form of dialogue in poetry between the two lovers. This is the form of the original text. Modern commentators emphasise this aspect of the poetry. The mystics who interpret the Canticle also have their place. A celebration of human love leads them to speak of the Canticle as a song celebrating God's love for us. Simone Weil (+1943) said of using human, sexual love as a way of speaking about God's love, that if we did not use human language then we would be like an artist trying to paint without brushes and paint. So both belong. We begin with the study of the Song as it is written, celebrating the life of love of the bride and bridegroom. This is the original meaning of the text. But as any writer, artist or poet knows, others take their own meaning from it. Literary theory speaks of the text and then of the reader's production of the meaning of the text. The text speaks of the love between bride and bridegroom while the mystics share their reflections on the Canticle and how they see God's love in Christ symbolized by the love between the bride and bridegroom in the Canticle.

The Canticle Itself:

The opening verses of the Canticle fly in the face of conventions of the ancient Middle East. The woman enters the stage and expresses her desire to be loved and kissed. This was not the done thing in public. In 8:1 she says she wished her beloved were her brother because, then, she could kiss him without any public reproach.

TITLE AND PROLOGUE

The Song of Songs, which is Solomon's.

The Bride
    Let him kiss me with the kisses of his mouth.
    Your love is more delightful than wine;
    delicate is the fragrance of your perfume,
    your name is an oil poured out,

and that is why the maidens love you.
Draw me in your footsteps, let us run.
The King has brought me into his rooms;
you will be our joy and our gladness.
We shall praise your love above wine;
how right it is to love you.

FIRST POEM

The Bride
I am black but lovely, daughters of Jerusalem,
like the tents of Kedar,
like the pavilions of Salmah.
Take no notice of my swarthiness,
it is the sun that has burnt me.
My mother's sons turned their anger on me,
they made me look after the vineyards.
Had I only looked after my own!

Tell me then, you whom my heart loves:
Where will you lead your flock to graze,
where will you rest it at noon?

(Canticle 1:1-7)

The woman expresses her yearning for the kisses of her beloved who is addressed in the third and second person. She expresses the intoxicating effect of love (1:2,4; 4:10). The identification of the man as king is a literary fiction. It is common to speak of lovers as being either a king or a queen to the beloved. The daughters of Jerusalem serve as a foil throughout the canticle so that the woman can develop the theme of love (cf 2:7; 5:8,16; 8:4). The vineyard motif (1:5; 6:11; 7:13; 8:11-12) suggests she is alluding to herself as the true vineyard given to her lover. The theme of the vineyard is found throughout the Bible. It can mean metaphorically the people of God (e.g. Isa 5:1-7; Mk 12:1; Mt 21:33).

The bride and bridegroom show us the enduring miracle that is love. They, the couple without names, stand for all couples who are in love.

If love exists (and it does) then God exists. The prophet Jeremiah, in another context, speaks of the "shout of joy and rejoicing and mirth, the voices of the bridegroom and bride" (Jer 7:34).

Thus the Canticle begins with the bride's longing for love. When we read the Canticle as a longing of Israel for God, it begins with Israel's longing and the Lord's desirability. As St. Augustine said: "You have made us for yourself, and our hearts are restless till they rest in you". God's Spirit and grace form the atmosphere in which the people of God move and have their being. In the Gospel of John, Jesus reveals God's glory. Viewed in a Christian way, the Canticle points to our hope of a life in union with God. The use of human imagery in the Song shows us we need not only God but the created other. We find love in the other. This can lead us to true intimacy with God. A child discovers love in the smile of its mother. Then the child grows and reaches out to others. This love opens the child to the love of God. Sadly many suffer from the lack of love from parents and those around them and they suffer much in life.

Canticle 1:9-17 is a long poem. The verses are strings of compliments. The woman asks for a noon rendezvous with her lover who is now in the role of a shepherd. His true feelings are expressed in his description of the bride's beauty and her finery is compared to Pharaoh's chariots. She responds by praising his intimacy and charm (symbolised by the henna and myrrh which he brings to her).

> That I may no more wander like a vagabond
> beside the flocks of your companions.

The Chorus
> If you do not know this, O loveliest of women,
> follow the tracks of the flock,
> and take your kids to graze
> close by the shepherds' tents.

The Bridegroom
> To my mare harnessed to Pharaoh's chariot
> I compare you, my love.

Your cheeks show fair between their pendants
and your neck within its necklaces.
We shall make you golden earrings
and beads of silver.

Dialogue of the Bride and Bridegroom
– While the King rests in his own room
my nard yields its perfume.
My Beloved is a sachet of myrrh
lying between my breasts.
My Beloved is a cluster of henna flowers
among the vines of Engedi.

– How beautiful you are, my love,
how beautiful you are!
Your eyes are doves.

– How beautiful you are, my Beloved,
and how delightful!
All green is our bed.

(Canticle 1:9-17)

Here the woman longs for a rendezvous with her beloved. His true feelings are expressed when he compares her finery to Pharoah's chariotry. She responds by praising his charm which his presence brings her.

The Lord's election of his people was neither a rational decision nor an arbitrary one. He loved her. She was beautiful in his eyes. What is true of Israel is true of the individual whom God loves. In Isa 43:4 we read "…you are precious in my eyes, because you are honoured and I love you". This is true of the bride and bridegroom. It is true of Israel and God. It is true of all people because we read: "…God so loved the world he gave his only Son" (Jn 3:16). We are the ones God loves. In 2:1-7 we see the lovers lovesick but happy. The woman's lover is a fruit tree among forest trees. She delights in his shade and loves to taste its fruit.

The man has brought his beloved into a place of love, a "love-house".
She is sick with love.

> – The beams of our house are of cedar,
> the panelling of cypress.

> – I am the rose of Sharon,
> the lily of the valleys.
> – As a lily among the thistles,
> so is my love among the maidens.
> – As an apple tree among the trees of the orchard,
> so is my Beloved among the young men.
> In his longed-for shade I am seated
> and his fruit is sweet to my taste.
> He has taken me to his banquet hall,
> and the banner he raises over me is love.
> Feed me with raisin cakes,
> restore me with apples,
> for I am sick with love.

> His left arm under my head,
> his right embraces me.

> – I charge you,
> daughters of Jerusalem,
> by the gazelles, by the hinds of the field,
> not to stir my love, nor rouse it,
> until it please to awake.

(Canticle 2:1-7)

The duet of mutual admiration continues in these verses. The
bridegroom compares the bride to the flowers of the plain of Sharon.
The dialogue closes with a sudden turn to the daughters in what seems
to be a refrain (5:8; 8:3-4). She describes her lover's embrace and issues
an admonition to them not to arouse love "until it please". Love is not
to be artificial or calculated. It has its own seasons for growth.

Bernard of Clairvaux said: "Uniquely among the trees of the forest, the Lord Jesus is a tree who bears fruit, and that according to his humanity".[2] Could we describe Israel and ourselves as lovesick for the Lord. The Targum at the parallel passage at 5:8 says: "The assembly of Israel said: 'I adjure you, O prophets..., if the merciful one should reveal himself to you, tell him that I am sick for his love'" (Targum). Origen of Alexandria says the Bride "feels herself wounded by the darts of love" when she "has been pierced through by the lovable javelin of knowing him"...[3] she has no desire now except for her beloved. The heart is the seat of love, but it is in our body and in our lives that we make this love incarnate. We have seen the beginnings of a very free expression of love. The desire for each other is intense. She is weak with lovesickness. Now the bride hears her lover's voice in 2:8-17 and in 3:1-5. He is like a gazelle or a young stag in his energy and desire to be with her. He stands outside and calls her to go into the country with him to enjoy the beauty of Spring as nature erupts after the passing of winter. Verses 2:8-17 is one of my favourite passages in the Bible. If there was a form of 'Desert Island Bible Passages', then this would be one of the passages I would keep. Desert Island Discs is a BBC radio show where the guest brings along the records he or she would have with him or her if they were marooned on a desert island.

> I hear my Beloved.
> See how he comes
> like a young stag.
> See where he stands
> behind our wall.
> He looks in at the window,
> he peers through the lattice.

> My Beloved lifts up his voice,
> he says to me,

[2] see Bernard of Clairvaux, On the Song of Songs, trans. Kilian Walsh and Irene M. Edmunds, The Works of Bernard of Clairvaux, vols. 1-4 (Kalamazoo, MI: 1971-1980), 48:4, written as Bernard in text.

[3] see Richard A. Norris (ed.), The Song of Songs: Interpreted by Early Christian and Medieval Commentators (Grand Rapids: 2003).

'Come then, my love,
my lovely one, come.
For see, winter is past,
the rains are over and gone.
The flowers appear on the earth.
The season of glad songs has come,
the cooing of the turtledove is heard
in our land.
The fig tree is forming its first figs
and the blossoming vines give out their fragrance.
Come then, my love,
my lovely one, come.
My dove, hiding in the clefts of the rock,
in the coverts of the cliff,
show me your face,
let me hear your voice;
for your voice is sweet
and your face is beautiful.'

Catch the foxes for us,
the little foxes
that make havoc of the vineyards,
for our vineyards are in flower.

My Beloved is mine and I am his.
He pastures his flock among the lilies.

Before the dawn-wind rises,
before the shadows flee,

(Canticle 2:8-17)

The bridegroom tells the bride to go with him. He describes the wonder of new life in the Spring. He speaks of blossoms, singing, figs and vines in bloom. The winter is past. She says "My beloved is mine, and I his". The are united in love. She warns of the 'foxes'. Our love can be threatened by others. The comparison of the lover to a gazelle evokes the freedom and homelessness of beasts in the first garden. The love of the bride and bridegroom is a form of Eden, a Paradise.

In the allegorical interpretation where the Lord is there is Paradise. Where the Lord comes in the reading of the Torah, or the celebration of the Eucharist, or in any way we come to know his presence, something of the final and intended fulfillment of all creation opens to our experience. We find ourselves at the gates of Heaven. In the Book of Revelation we hear the Lord say: "Behold I stand at the door and knock" (Rev 3:20). We are sought for by God like the bride desires the bridegroom. In the Targum we read how the Lord "jumped over one hundred and ninety years of slavery on account of the righteousness of the Matriarchs, who are compared to hills. He looked in through the windows and peered through the lattices, and he saw the blood of the Passover sacrifice… and when it was morning he said to me, 'Rise up, congregation of Israel, my darling from of old'".

Origen says: "The Church first recognises Christ only by his voice. For he sends his voice by the prophets. And for a time the Bride, that is the Church… heard only his voice, until the time when she saw him with her eyes".[4] In another place he says, putting words into the incarnate Christ: "Arise… my dove, for behold the winter is past… By rising from the dead, I have quelled the tempest and restored peace".[5]

The love of the bride and bridegroom is pure, but so often our own love is not pure and we suffer and cause others to suffer because of our selfishness. The love in the Song of Songs shows us that love is good and life-giving. It points us beyond our selfishness to seek pure love, the pure love that is God. Then our 'winter' of love will pass and we will find new life in the Spring.

In 3:1-5 we hear what appears to be a dream sequence. The lover is the maiden's obsession night and day. So in a dream she seeks him. She goes about at night querying those she meets about her beloved. She finds him and will not let him go until she has brought him to her mother's home. In love between humans there are often times of loss and anxiety.

[4] Origen, The Song of Songs: Commentary and Homilies, trans. R.P. Larson, Ancient Christian Writers, vol. 26 (Westminster MD: 1947) p. 208.
[5] op. cit, p. 302.

On my bed, at night, I sought him
whom my heart loves.
I sought but did not find him.
So I will rise and go through the City;
in the streets and the squares
I will seek him whom my heart loves.
… I sought but did not find him.

The watchmen came upon me
on their rounds in the City;
'Have you seen him whom my heart loves?'

Scarcely had I passed them
than I found him whom my heart loves.
I held him fast, nor would I let him go
till I had brought him
into my mother's house,
into the room of her who conceived me.

The Bridegroom
    I charge you,
    daughters of Jerusalem,
    by the gazelles, by the hinds of the field,
    not to stir my love, nor rouse it,
    until it please to awake.

(Canticle 3:1-5)

This unit forms a kind of double with 5:2-6 where the loss and search are repeated. 3:1-5 is marked by repetitions: 'seek', 'find', 'whom my heart loves'. The themes of presence and absence are common in love poetry. The woman finds her lover and peace is restored.

In the Targum we read:

"But when the people of the House of Sarah saw that… [the presence of God] had been taken from them, and they had been left in darkness as in the night, they sought… but did not find. Then the children of Sarah said one to another, 'Let us arise and go around to the Tent of meeting which Moses has pitched outside the camp... and seek the holy presence that has departed from us".

(Targum)

St. Bernard of Clairvaux said: "Who is it whom your soul loves...? Has he no name...?" The woman lacks a name for her beloved because "The holy love that is the matter of the Song cannot be expressed by words" (Bernard of Clairvaux, op. cit, 79.1).

Many blunder around our world in search of love, we can pray that the great lover that is God will find a way into the lives of the lonely people searching for love.

In 4:1-7 the lover praises the beauty of his beloved. This is what the ancient near-east called a wasf. This is where the woman or the man describes the beauty of the beloved. It might not go down too well in a modern context if the lover said to his beloved "your hair is like a flock of goats" or "your teeth are like a flock of shorn ewes".

The Bridegroom
How beautiful you are, my love,
how beautiful you are!
Your eyes, behind your veil,
are doves;
your hair is like a flock of goats
frisking down the slopes of Gilead.
Your teeth are like a flock of shorn ewes
as they come up from the washing.
Each one has its twin,
not one unpaired with another.
Your lips are a scarlet thread
and your words enchanting.
Your cheeks, behind your veil,
are halves of pomegranate.
Your neck is the tower of David

built as a fortress,
hung round with a thousand bucklers,
and each the shield of a hero.
Your two breasts are two fawns, twins of a gazelle,
that feed among the lilies.

Before the dawn-wind rises,
before the shadows flee,
I will go to the mountain of myrrh,
to the hill of frankincense.

You are wholly beautiful, my love,
and without a blemish.

(Canticle 4:1-7)

The wasf, praise of the beauty of the beloved, was a common form of poetry at that time (see W. Hermann, ZAW 73 (1963), p. 176-197). The pomegranate is like an orange and he uses this to refer to the bride. He accepts the call of the bride to come to her.

The Lord tells Israel that she is beautiful and that he loves her. What God says to Israel she says to all. "You are beautiful in my eyes and honoured and I love you" (Isa 43:4). In 3:6 - 5:1, we have the description of the morning of the wedding group (3:6-11) when the voice of the bridegroom is heard praising the beauty of his be loved (4:1-15). He is struck by her beauty and is very much in love.

In 5:2 - 6:3 we hear a kind of flash-back where the bride seeks the bridegroom when he is apparently lost. All love has its moments of crisis, and growth. "Say to my love that I am sick with love" (Canticle 5:8).

In 6:4 - 8:4 we find more love poems. There is a celebration of the love of the bride by the bridegroom (6:4 - 7:9) and of the bridegroom by the bride (7:10 - 8:3). The bride speaks of going into the countryside to enjoy the fragrances of nature and Spring (7:12-14). She regrets that in the society in which she lives she cannot publicly express her love for the beloved (8:2).

In 8:5-7, we have the epilogue to the Canticle. The bride speaks of her lover coming from the desert. This refers to 3:6. The apple tree she refers to is a symbol of love. She speaks of the love that unites them. "Love is as strong as death". True love conquers obstacles and sustains us in life. It gives us meaning. The woman tells that love (her love) is divine and a flame of Yahweh himself. In the first letter of St. John we read: "There is no fear in love. But perfect love drives out fear, because fear has to do with punishment. The one who fears is not perfect in love" (1 Jn 4:18). This is the love we seek. St. Paul says: "...God shows his love for us in that while we were still sinners Christ died for us" (Rom 5:8). The resurrection of Jesus showed that love is stronger than death. Jesus is God's word made flesh (Jn 1:14) and his word is love:

The Chorus
        Who is this coming up from the desert
        leaning on her Beloved?

The Bridegroom
        I awakened you under the apple tree,
        there where your mother conceived you,
        there where she who gave birth to you conceived you.

        Set me like a seal on your heart,
        like a seal on your arm.
        For love is strong as Death,
        jealousy relentless as Sheol.
        The flash of it is a flash of fire,
        a flame of Yahweh himself.
        Love no flood can quench,
        no torrents drown.
                                          (Canticle 8:5-7)

The image of the "seal" that the woman uses conveys her desire for the constant presence of the lover with her. She compares love to death and sheol. These were for the biblical writers signs of unrelenting power since no one escapes them. True love ('ahaba) and ardour (qin'a) will prevail just as surely. The fiery quality of love is said to be in Hebrew as alhebetya, a flame of Yahweh. The fire of love is a fire of Yahweh, a participation in the Lord's white hot love. She speaks of the deep waters, the torrents. These cannot drown love. The phrase conjures images of the power of the sea and the Abyss (see Isa 43:2; 51:10). The power of love is beyond any price. In Romans 5:5 Paul speaks of this perfect love being poured into our hearts by the Holy Spirit given us.

In the Targum we read: "Many floods cannot quench love. This is the love which the Holy One, blessed be he, has for Israel". God's love is victorious "O death, where is your sting? O grave, where is your victory" (1 Cor 15:55). Jesus' resurrection is his victory over death and he is now glorified at the right hand of the Father. He lives forever interceding for us so that we can join him in the perfect union of love in the power of the Holy Spirit. His resurrection is the cause of our hope. St. Bernard of Clairvaux said: "He loved us before we existed; and went beyond that to love us when we resisted him... Indeed had he not loved his enemies, he would have no friends" (Bernard 20:2). Augustine wrote: "Just as death achieves heights of fury in the work of destruction, so love achieves heights of fury in the work of salvation" (Norris).

In the resurrection Jesus now lives and will die no more. He is present to us and our journey is to come to know him. He calls us to be united with him in love by the power of the Holy Spirit. In this way we give glory to the Father. The glory of God is a human being fully alive (St. Ireneus). Jesus came so that we could have life to the full (Jn 10:10).

In the Book of the Apocalypse John uses the image of a bride to symbolise the new creation. All our history points to our hope of the final victory of God. In Revelation we read: "Then I saw a new heaven and a new earth, the first heaven and the first earth had disappeared now, and there was no longer any sea. I saw the holy city, the new Jerusalem, coming down from God out of heaven, as beautiful as a bride adorned for her husband" (Ap 21:1f). The new heaven and the new earth comes from Is 65:17-25. This is a new creation. The disappearance of the sea is equivalent to the eternal confinement and punishment of the dragon, the beast ('antichrist') and the false prophet (19:20; 20:10) and to the elimination of death and Hades (20:14). The elimination of the sea symbolises the complete victory of creation over chaos, of life over death. It is in this new creation that God will wipe away "all tears from their eyes; there will be no more death, and no more mourning or sadness. The world of the past has gone" (Ap 21:4). The image of the new creation as a bride calls to mind the love-poetry of the Canticle of Canticles and the language of love between bride and bridegroom.

The Cistercian Renewal:

There was a renewal in the life of the Church in the 12th century, led by Monastic reforms. Among these were the Cistercians. The order's founding fathers, led by St. Robert of Molesme (1028-1111), were a group of Benedictine monks from the Abbey of Molesme. They were dissatisfied with the relaxed observance of the rule of St. Benedict in their abbey. They decided to live a solitary life under the strictest interpretation of the rule. Robert was succeeded by Stephen Harding, who proved to be the real organiser of the Cistercian rule and order. They founded an abbey at Citeaux (Latin: Cistercium) a locality in Burgundy, near Dijon. This happened in 1098.

Their monastery was a return to the ancient tradition of the monks. Rather than utilising feudal labour, the Cistercians made use of conversi, lay-brothers, to till their lands. This development opened up the monastic life, albeit in a more simplified fashion than that observed by the choir monks, to a whole new social class, since the conversi were uneducated workers. In the writings of many of the great Cistercians the Song of Songs played a large part in their lives. One of the great figures of this reform was Bernard of Clairvaux (1090-1153). In the first of his sermons for the dedication of a Church, he said

> What is more wonderful than when one who could scarcely for two days refrain from lust, from intoxication, from drunkenness, wantonness, impurity, and other similar and dissimilar vices, now refrains from them for many years, and even for life? What greater miracle than when so many youths, adolescents, nobles – all those I see here – are

bound, as in an open prison without chains, riveted only by the fear of God in order to endure penance so severe that it is beyond human power, above nature, out of the ordinary? ... What are these save evident proofs of the Holy Spirit living within you? The body's lively movements prove the soul dwells there; spiritual life proves the Spirit dwells in the soul. The former is recognised by sight and hearing; the latter from charity, humility and other virtues.

(Bernard 5:371-372:2)

The monks sought silence so that they could respond to God. They wished to be part of God's creative and redeeming love. They saw all of creation as being the work of God.

Bernard of Clairvaux:

Dante speaks of Bernard in the Divina Commedia:
tal era io mirando la vivace
carità di colui, che 'n questo mondo,
contemplando, gustò di quella pace.

(Such was I, gazing on the living
charity of him who, in this world,
in contemplation tasted of that peace).
Paradiso 31, 109-111

The Cistercian mystic also serves as the poet's teacher:

Affetto al suo piacer, quel contemplante
libero officio di dottore assunse,
e cominciò queste parole sante.

(With his love fixed on his delight, that contemplator
freely assumed the office of a teacher,
and began these holy words.)
Paradiso 32, 1-3

Dante was not alone among the medieval writers in considering Bernard of Clairvaux (1090-1153) the supreme guide to the heights of heavenly contemplation. Bernard was a twelfth-century mystic. He was a Cistercian in the Abbey of Clairvaux, yet he got involved in many issues of the time: he helped restore peace when there was a papal schism, he reacted against Abelard and his theological, philosophical method and he was a leading preacher in drumming up support for the second crusade. The two latter events, Abelard and the crusade, and Bernard's input, are matters of controversy to this day.

Bernard was the son of Tescelin and Aleth, daughter of the Lord of Montbard. He was born in the family castle of Fontaines, near Dijon in Burgundy. He was well-educated. Bernard was sent to Chatillon-on-the-Seine to study in a college of secular canons. During this period his mother died and this threw Bernard into a state of prolonged and acute depression.

He became attracted to the monastery of Citeaux which had been founded fifteen years before. He prayed about this and finally entered the monastery at Citeaux. He brought a large number of his family with him – thirty one to be precise.

When they arrived at Citeaux, near Easter, 1112, there had been no new novices for several years and Stephen Harding, the abbot, was thrilled to welcome them. Bernard, because of his health, was given light work and he devoted himself to prayer. The Cistercians chose swampy, unproductive lands, but their work transformed these swampy areas into fertile fields. The Count of Troyes offered a site on his estate for a new monastery. Bernard was put in charge of this new foundation in the diocese of Langres, in Champagne: the land was poor and the monks lived through a period of extreme hardship. Bernard, at first, was severe in discipline, but he saw that the monks became discouraged. He relaxed his discipline and made the monastery more human. He started to preach and he began to make sure that the monks got proper food. The fame of the abbot and the monastery spread throughout France. The monastery was given the name of Clairvaux. Bernard suffered from anxiety and had frequent stomach problems. In 1118 he became so ill his life was in danger. One of the powerful bishops of the time, William of Champeaux, obtained permission to look after Bernard for a period of twelve months. Knowing that Bernard needed rest and quiet he placed him in a little house outside the monastery enclosure at Clairvaux and there he rested and became strong. Bernard returned to the monastery but the order directed him to devote himself to preaching and writing. His work of preaching led to travel throughout Europe. His life, he said, was "overrun everywhere by anxieties, suspicion, cares. There is hardly an hour free from the crowd of discordant applicants, and the troubles and cares of their business. I have no power to stop them coming and cannot refuse to see them, and they do not leave me even time to pray".

Bernard's writings included 'The Steps of Humility and Pride' and 'On Loving God'. In 1135 he began his mystical masterpiece, 'The Sermons on the Song of Songs'. This was a work he spent the rest of his life working on.

Bernard said of Jesus, "He offered his flesh to those who knew flesh so that through it they may know spirit too" (Bernard, 1;27). Bernard concentrated on the personal meaning of the Song of Songs as telling the love between Christ and the individual Christian. The first verse of the Song says: "Let him kiss me with the kisses of his mouth – for your love is more delightful than wine" (Canticle 1:1). Bernard said there must be multiple kisses between the soul and God. The kisses comprise the whole course of salvation history – longing for Christ among the just souls of the Old Testament, the kiss of the Incarnation, Christ bringing redemption to humanity in the present and the hearty kiss of the future eschatological time.

Bernard was a great advocate of Lectio Divina. He and the monks would read a text, meditate on its meaning and then form a prayer of what they had read. Bernard's reading of the Song of Songs was spiritual. This was his production of the meaning of the text for him. He also saw the monks as bringing out different aspects of God's salvation. Once a monk came to him who complained he was dry of any spiritual feeling. Bernard told him his place was with those who longed for Christ's coming and he was to pray in that condition. The monk went away consoled.

In Sermon 7 on the Song of Songs the kiss is identified with the Holy Spirit, the bond of love, the bond of union between the Father and the Son (see Sermon 8). In Sermon 4 Bernard describes how we coin human, anthropomorphic descriptions of God:

> "God has a mouth by which he teaches humanity knowledge, a hand by which he provides nourishment to all flesh, he has feet whose footstool is earth... God has all these things, I say, 'not naturally, but effectively', that is by reason of what he does"
>
> (Bernard 1:20)

This is why Bernard feels he can use the words of human love in the Song to speak of God.

We can become slaves of the world we see, of the flesh, to use a phrase of Bernard's. He goes on to say we must see beyond the world and its appearance so that we can come to know the world of the Spirit. It is in this world that God has come to speak to us.

> Woe! Thus human beings lost and changed their glory for the likeness of a grass-eating beast (Ps 105:20)! God had mercy on their errors and deigned to come forth from the shady dark mountain [i.e., of his hidden divinity] and place his tabernacle in the sun [i.e., take on flesh in the Incarnation]. He offered his flesh to those who knew flesh so that through it they might come to know spirit too. While he was in the flesh, through the flesh he performed works not of the flesh but of God...
>
> (Bernard 1.27.11-15)

We have, then, almost a syllogistic argument – a Bernardine equivalent of Anselm's famous proof for the necessity of the God-man in the Cur Deus Homo? (Why did God become man?).

God does not have a body of any kind.
But, humanity's fallen state means that we are all enslaved to the body.

Therefore, salvation is impossible unless God takes on a body.

For Bernard Jesus is the God-man, and is lovable on firstly the purely human level: "If he had not drawn near, he would not draw [us] to himself, and if he had not drawn himself, he would not have drawn [us] out of sin" (Bernard, 2.26.3). The sweetness of this love in Christ is needed in order to drive out the wrongful loves we experience and allow the true love of God to reign in our hearts. We learn love by gazing on the human-being Jesus and how the fulness of divinity lives in him (Col 2:9).

Bernard saw Jesus as the Word of the Father made flesh (Jn 1:14). He was influenced by Paul and Augustine. He, the Word made flesh, is the source of our strength and by the power of the Holy Spirit this love transforms us. We are transformed by love as we conform our lives to the Word made flesh. Bernard was very fond of the Biblical text, 2 Corinthians 3:18; "All of us, gazing upon the Lord's glory with revealed face, are transformed into the same image from glory to glory, as if by the Spirit of the Lord".

God became human so that we could become God. What was relatively new was Bernard's starting point. He placed great emphasis on the humanity of Christ and the saving events of God in the life of Jesus the Christ. Bernard constantly calls up for his reader the major events of the life of Christ.

He was incomprehensible and inaccessible, invisible and completely unthinkable. Now he wishes to be comprehended, wishes to be seen, wishes to be thought about. How, you ask? As lying in the manger, resting in the Virgin's lap, preaching on the mountain, praying through the night, or hanging on the cross, growing pale in death, free among the dead and ruling in hell, and also as rising on the third day, showing the apostles the place of the nails, the sings of victory, and finally as ascending over heaven's secrets in their sight.

(Bernard 5.282.19-25)

Bernard's role in the development of the devotion to the sacred humanity of Christ, especially the mysteries of the nativity, as well as the passion, has been much stressed by students of medieval religion. He is also known for fostering such affective practices as devotion to the sacred name of Jesus. The account given here shows just how significant the carnal love of Christ in all its stages was for the abbot. Nevertheless, for Bernard such carnal love was always just the beginning of the itinerary that was meant to lead to spiritual love. To neglect the higher form of love would be to fail to do justice to Bernard's thought. This is why the Resurrection, and even more the Ascension, on which the abbot preached more often than any other mystery and which he honoured by instituting a special liturgical procession, were such special feasts for him. To cite his own words:

> To clarify what I said, if my Lord Jesus had risen from the grave but had not ascended to heaven, it could not have been said of him that he "passed beyond" (pertransierat), but only that he "passed from" (transierat)... Therefore, to believe in the Resurrection is to pass from; to believe in the Ascension is to pass beyond... Our Head preceded both those souls [the seekers referred to in Song 3:4] and the other members of his Body on earth in two issues – his Resurrection, as we said, and his Ascension. These are the "first fruits of Christ" (1 Cor 15:23). But if he precedes, so does our faith, for where does it not follow him?
>
> (Bernard 2.273.20-274.7)

Bernard spoke of love in his writings. He said:

> "Of all the motions, senses and affections of the soul it is love alone in which the creature is able, even if not on an equal basis, to repay to its Creator for what it has received, to weigh back something from the same measure."
>
> (Bernard 2:300.28f)

Bernard was very influenced by certain scripture texts which he meditated on and these texts appear in his writings. Among them are

Matt 11:33, 1 Jn 4:8,14; 1 Cor 6:17; 2 Cor 3:18; Phil 3:20f. He spent many years meditating and writing on the Song of Songs, a work which was not completed at his death. He came to know the love of God and he holds out hope for God's mercy for those who feel weighed down by sin and failure "is able to find in itself not only a source from which it may seek to breathe in hope of pardon, in hope of mercy, but also whence it may dare to aspire to the nuptials of the Word" (Bernard 2.298.20-21). We are both forgiven and accepted but we are called to live in union with Christ by the gift of the Holy Spirit. We are called to life. He cautions us to take our growth in the life of the Spirit step by step. We are led into our life with God. Each way to God is unique to the individual and is always conducted at the discretion of the Holy Spirit.

The presence of God is something Bernard reflected on in his writings. The Divine Lover is present to us in a variety of ways, God dwells in every soul as a special heaven of its own according to the capacity of its love (Bernard 1:19.3-5). As the soul grows in love towards the goal of the freedom of the Spirit it becomes a happier place for the indwelling of God, and it becomes more sensitive to the working of God in our lives. One comes to know "the presence of the Benefactor and Giver himself as far as possible while one is in the weak body" (Bernard, 1:187-189). This grace is not given to all. To those who experience this presence he describes the coming of the Word (Verbum) as spouse (see Sermons in Bernard 75:5-7).

Early in his Sermon on the Song of Songs, Bernard spoke of the role of Trinity in the soul's prayers. He referred to Song 1:1. The kiss of the mouth is identified with the Holy Spirit, understood as the mutual kiss or bond between the Father and the Son, who is breathed forth by the risen Christ upon the Apostles (Sermon 8:1-2). The bride's longing, then, is a desire for the Holy Spirit, the love and goodness of the Father and Son, whose coming brings the soul the gifts of knowledge and love that delights the reason and the will. This coming constitutes the 'kiss of the kiss', that is, of the Holy Spirit. The Son raises and heals reason so that it can judge for itself in order to produce humility, while the Holy Spirit visits and purifies the will to give birth to charity. Finally the

Father unites to himself "as glorious Bride the soul that is without stain through humility and without spot through charity, so that will does not war with reason nor does reason deceive will" (on Humility in Bernard 3:22.27-33.7). The Son brings us to strict truth through the work of humility, the Holy Spirit grants devout truth, and the Father "pure truth" through the rapture of contemplation.

He reflects on the nature of ecstasy and rapture in the Steps of Humility and Pride (see 8:22-23) and stresses the gratuitous character of any ascent to the third heaven of Paul (see 2 Cor 2:12) where the Father is to be found. It is interesting that the same texts (Song 1:3 and Song 3:4) that Bernard used in Sermon 23 to express the union between the Word as bridegroom and his friends is used here to describe the union between the soul and the Father.

Most of Bernard's references to the divine presence concern the individual persons of the Trinity. Following Sermon 8 he speaks of the presence and work of the Holy Spirit. We can perceive, in some cases, the Spirit within us crying out "Abba, Father" (Gal 4:6; Rom 8:15 see Sermon 8:9). We are called to be sensitive to the work of the Holy Spirit and to act according to the Spirit's will (Bernard 1:98-99). We experience joy in the presence of the Holy Spirit. Other times Bernard says we experience more the presence of the Word. Other times the Father.

In the seventy-fourth of the Sermons on the Song of Songs, Bernard calls on the Bridegroom to return as the Bride does in Song 2:7. He models his writing on Paul's chapter twelve of the Second Letter to the Corinthians. He says, speaking of his own experience:

> Now bear with my foolishness a little while (2 Cor 11:1). I want to tell you as I promised about my own experience of this sort of thing. Not that it is important (2 Cor 12:1), but I am relating it to be helpful. If you profit from it, I shall be consoled for my foolishness. If not, I will proclaim my foolishness. I admit that the Word has also come to me, and – I speak foolishly (2 Cor 11:17) – come often. As often as

he has come to me, I have not perceived the different times of his coming. I perceived that he has been present (adesse sensi); I remembered that he had been there. Sometimes I was able to anticipate his coming, but I never felt it, nor his departing either. Even now I admit that I don't know whence he came into my soul and where he went after he left it, and by what way he entered and left.

(Bernard, 2:242:13-22)

We find ourselves in Jesus, in the Word made flesh (Jn 1:14). His presence can "be sensed, perceived or felt only by the happy individual in whom the Word dwells, who lives for him, who is moved by him" (Bernard 2:243.19-20). Bernard in referring to the Word is referring to the Word of God who came among us. John's Gospel begins

"In the beginning was the Word,
The Word was with God
And the Word was God.
He was with God in the beginning
Through him all things came to be,
not one thing had its being but through him.
All that came to be had life in him
and that life was the light of men,
A light that shines in the dark,
A light that darkness could not overpower."

(Jn 1:1-4)

and later

"The Word was made flesh,
he lived among us,
And we saw his glory,
the glory that was his as the Son of the Father,
full of grace and truth."

(Jn 1:14)

Verse 1 recalls Genesis 1:1 at the beginning of creation. It also recalls the tradition of Wisdom being at the side of God when he created the world (Prov 8:30, Wisdom 7:25). He, the Word, is one with God, and through the word of God all things came to be. He is the light that shines in the darkness.

In 1:14 we read of the Word becoming flesh, that is in the person of Jesus. This harks back to the Old Testament image of divine glory and Wisdom dwelling with Israel (Ex 25:8-9, Joel 3:17, Zech 2:10, Ez 43:7). The "son of God" is to dwell with Israel forever (Sir 24:4-8, 10), God's mercy and lovingkindness (hesed we'emet) to his people is found in Jesus who is the incarnation of God's love. Jesus died and rose again and Bernard is a witness in his writings to the real presence of Jesus in the life of the soul. He came to know Jesus by engaging in a life of prayer. His coming to know Jesus is both dynamic and relational. His work speaks of his experience of knowing God the Father, the Son (the Word made flesh) and the Holy Spirit. His writings communicate his experience and help point us to finding our own path in the life of the Spirit. Not all are called to mystical raptures or visions but all are called, each in a unique way. All are gifted and we are all called to build one another up in the Spirit.

The link between prayer and the Holy Spirit is seen in John's Gospel by the link between the person praying and Jesus the Christ. Jesus is the one who possesses the fulness of the Spirit. The Holy Spirit lives in Him and he gives the Spirit without measure (Jn 3:36). Jesus and the Spirit form the place of encounter for the believer with God. In Chapter 7 of John is the source of the Spirit. Jesus says: "Whoever believes in me, may come and drink. For scripture says 'Rivers of living waters will flow from his side'" (Jn 7:38). This recalls the water flowing from the Temple in Ezekiel 47. In Jn 14:16 Jesus says that after he goes he will send the Paraclete, the consoler (Jn 14:16). This Spirit lives in the heart of the disciples, those who welcome the Word of God (Jn 14:17f). In the letter of John we read:

> "Dear friends, let us love one another, for love comes from God. Everyone who loves has been born of God and knows God. Whoever does not love does not know God, because God is love. This is how God showed his love among us: He

sent his one and only Son into the world that we might have life through him. This is love: not that we loved God, but that he loved us and sent his Son as an atoning sacrifice for our sins. Dear friends, since God has loved us, we also ought to love one another. No one has ever seen God, but if we love one another, God lives in us and his love is made complete in us. This is how we know we live in him and he in us: He has given us his Spirit. And we have seen and testify that the Father has sent his son to be the saviour of the world. If anyone acknowledges that Jesus is the Son of God, God lives in them and they in God. And so we know and rely on the love God has for us. God is love. Whoever lives in love lives in God and God in them."

(1 Jn 4:7-16)

In this section the letter of John tells us that Jesus shows us God's love. Love distinguishes the person from the one who knows God and the one who does not (cf 1 Jn 2:4-5; 3:1,11). God's love is revealed to the Christian in Jesus, but it can also be said to be revealed in the Christian community which now lives life through this love (John 5:26; 6:57 and 1 Jn 5:11). Jesus loved us first and gave his life for us. The Holy Spirit leads us into this love and we come to know and believe the love God has for us.

We can see how these themes resonated with Bernard and his teaching. He saw that Christ shows us God's love for us. When we come to know Christ, we know love. We are to show forth our experience of love in our communities. We live our life through love (see Jn 5:26; 6:57; 1 Jn 5:11). He loved us and he was sent by God to show us love (see Jn 1:16-18, 3:16f). God's love abides in the heart of those who love like Jesus. God is love (4:8). The gift of the Spirit means God lives in our hearts. He teaches us the love God has for us.

St. Bernard and Love:

Bernard experienced the love of God spoken about in John's writings. He lived in an atmosphere of love, that is, in the atmosphere of the Holy

Spirit. This is the secret for his success as a preacher and also for the success of the Cistercian reform. Many other monasteries were founded from Clairvaux and their influence spread right across Europe. They shared the spirit of Bernard. The Canticle speaks of the love between man and woman. When love is perfected it is divine and we share by the Holy Spirit, in the very life of God himself. Through Christ, living in us by the Holy Spirit, we come to love God and all things and all people in God.

Contemplation is a gaze of faith and love fixed on Jesus. It is silence and it is silent love. Our words of prayer lead to the kindling of love. Contemplative prayer is a communion of love in the Holy Spirit and it brings life to others. "To fall in love with God is the greatest romance; to seek him the greatest adventure; to find him the greatest human achievement."[6] Bernard said. "God... loves and has no other source save himself from which he loves. That is why he loves more ardently, because he does not so much possess love as he is love" (Bernard 1:173.16f). Bernard looked at the characteristics of God on the basis of Ephesians 3:18f;

> "...so that Christ may live in your hearts through faith and then, planted in love and built on love, you will have strength to understand with all the saints, the length, the breadth, the height and the depth; until knowing the love of Christ, which is beyond all knowledge, you are filled with the utter fullness of God. God's length is his eternity, his breadth the love that surpasses not only every affection, but also all knowledge"
>
> (Bernard 3:491:8f).

His height is his power, his depth his wisdom. Love is the law of God's being. He cannot do other than love.

His beauty is his love, all the greater because it was prior (*praeveniens*). The more she understands that she was loved

---

[6] see Raphael Simon, The Glory of Thy People: The Story of a Conversion (New Hope: 1985) p. xiii. This quote is attributed to St. Augustine.

before being a lover, the more and amply she cries out in her heart's core and with the voice of her deepest affections that she must love him. Thus, the Word's speaking is the giving of the gift, the soul's response is wonder and thanksgiving. The more she grasps that she is overcome in loving, the more she loves. The more she admits that he has gone before her, the more awestruck she is.

(Bernard 2:54.29-55.4)

In his work 'On Loving God' Bernard says that our human heart cannot be satisfied with anything short of God's love. "God is the reason for loving God; the measure of loving him is to love without measure" (Bernard 3:119,19). Our problem is we do not know this love. Our experiences of love can be hurtful and disappointing. We can be hurt in our search for love. Bernard points us to the fact that God is different and is all loving. In prayer and meditation and by contemplation we enter another space where there is only pure love. In our hearts lies the desire to experience this love.

...You are good, O Lord, to the soul that seeks you. What then in the case of the one that finds you? What is wonderful in this is that no one can seek you who has not first found you. Therefore, you wish to be found so that you may be sought, to be sought that you may be found. You can indeed seek and find, but you cannot be forestalled.

(Bernard 3:138.12-13)

Our loves on this earth can be seen as a shadow of that eternal love that is God. Bernard says in his Sermons on the Song of Songs:

"I set out different affections so that the one pertaining to the Bride may be clearer. A slave fears the Lord's face, a hireling hopes for his generosity. A disciple is attentive to his master; a son honours his father – but the one who seeks a kiss, she loves"

(Bernard 1:31.17-21)

The love of the bride for the bridegroom was the best image Bernard could think of to explain our longing for this infinite kiss, this infinite love.

> Love is a great thing, but there are degrees in it. The Bride is at the top. Children also love, but with thought to an inheritance.... I am suspicious of a love which seems to be supported by hope of gaining something else.... Pure love has no self-interest. Pure love does not take its power from hope, nor does it feel any kind of distrust. It belongs to the Bride, because this is what a Bride is. Her reality and her hope is one single love; she is rich in it and the Bridegroom is content with it. He is not looking for anything else; she has nothing else. This is why he is a Groom and she is the Bride. That is proper to them which no one else attains, not even a son.
>
> (Bernard 2:301.12-22)

This is how Bernard summed up the position of the Bride and points out to what defines her: the pure, disinterested and total character of her love. God is what he has – God does not possess love, but is love. Here Bernard follows Augustine. Bernard says: "a single soul, if she loves God, sweetly, visibly and vehemently, is a Bride" (Bernard 2:239.7-8).

God loved us first (1 Jn 4:8f), both in creating and redeeming us. Bernard would consider it wrong and against the life of grace if we did not love ourselves. We are the ones for whom Christ died.[7] The true issue is how we can love in an unselfish way. Love is what leads us to God and invites us to God now and in the next life. The capacity to know and to love are for Bernard the essential forms of human nature. Both these forms though fallen, can be restored by the saving work of Christ. "Christ illumines the intellect, the Holy Spirit purifies the affection" (Bernard 5:136:22f).

---

[7] Etienne Gilson, The Mystical Theology of St. Bernard (London: 1940) p. 116-18.

In Sermon 6 on the Ascension, he analyses Christ's activity. He shows us that by ascending into heaven, he intended to send the Holy Spirit to us "so that spiritual affection may be joined with spiritual understanding" (Bernard 5:159.3-4). It is in this love that we attain God in this life. Knowledge cannot on its own, but must be lifted up in love.

The love of which Bernard speaks is a marriage, because it is founded on a mutuality and reciprocity between the lovers that finds its closest analogy in human marriage (in an ideal form).

> Therefore, from what she possesses that belongs to God, the soul in love recognises and has no doubt that she is loved. This is the way it is – God's love gives birth to the soul's love and his prevenient intention makes the soul intent, full of care for him who cares for her. I do not know what closeness of nature it is that enables the soul, when once his face is revealed, to gaze upon God's glory and to be necessarily so quickly conformed to him and transformed into the same image (2 Cor 3:18). Therefore, in whatever way you get yourself ready for God, this is the way he will appear to you.
> (Bernard 2:206:20.2-6).

Bernard uses the idea of 'adhering' to God. In prayer we come to know God and live in union with him. Bernard speaks of a "marvelous and somehow inseparable mingling of the heavenly light and the enlightened mind. To adhere to God is to be one Spirit with him (1Cor 6:17)" (Bernard 1:9.19-20).

Bernard speaks of "the fundamental ways in which God can be seen in this life; first as manifested in all creatures; second as in the days of the patriarchs, shown through external images and spoken words; and finally by a divine gaze more different than these as it is more interior when God deigns through himself to visit the soul seeking him" (Bernard 1:221f).

Bernard speaks of receiving mystical graces. These witness to the activity of God on the soul, but the most important gift is the gift of love. In loving we come to know God, in so far as we are able (Sermon 50:6). In coming to know God we come to know ourselves as who we really are. We discover ourselves in God. We come to love ourselves and our neighbour as ourselves. We learn true love from our relationship with God, who is all-love. Bernard ends this sermon with an impassioned prayer:

> "Direct our actions as our temporal necessity demands and dispose our affections as your eternal truth requires so that each of us may safely boast in you and say that, 'He has ordered charity in me'."
>
> (Bernard 2:83.14-17)

"The soul that knows God sees things as if she alone is seen by God" (Bernard 2:207.9-10). God is infinite love and it seems to us, when we discover his love, that we exist as if we were the only person in the universe.

It is through contemplative prayer, in which the soul seeks Jesus and the Father through the Holy Spirit, that Saint Bernard was enabled to say:

> "Love is sufficient of itself, it gives pleasure by itself and because of itself. It is its own merit, its own reward. Love looks for no cause outside itself, no effect beyond itself. Its profit lies in its practice. I love because I love. I love that I may love. Love is a great thing so long as it continually returns to its fountainhead, flows back to its source, always drawing form there the water which continually replenishes it."
>
> (Sermon 83 on Song, Bernard 2:300f)

We become what we contemplate.

Chapter 5

The Divine Canticle of Saint John of the Cross

Born Juan de Yepes (1542-1591) in the little Castilian town of Fontiveros in 1542,[1] John was the son of Gonzalo de Yepes and Catalina Alvares. Catalina was a poor weaver probably of Moorish background and Gonzalo's family were wealthy silk merchants, originally of Jewish (converso) stock. Gonzalo's family disinherited him when he married Catalina. Gonzalo died when the young Juan was only two. Catalina had a difficult time and she moved to Medina del Campo to continue work as a weaver. There Juan was educated at a school for the poor. He worked helping in the local hospital. The administrator of the hospital, Don Alonso Alvares, found the young man an able nurse. He enrolled the young Juan in the local Jesuit school where he received a good education.

Rather than enter the Jesuits, in 1563 Juan elected to join the Carmelite order, which had recently established a house in Medina. Taking the name of John of St. Matthias, he spent a year of novitiate studying the Carmelite Rule before being sent off to the university at Salamanca to pursue philosophy and theology. He was enrolled in the Arts Faculty there for three years, and then in theology for 1567-68. We do not know exactly what courses he took, but Friar John received a good education. He was certainly familiar with Aristotle and other philosophers; he knew Thomas Aquinas, whose *Summa Theologiae* by this time was a major textbook in the universities, but there were a number of theological traditions taught in Salamanca. As a Carmelite, he would have become familiar with the thought of John Baconthorpe (d. 1348), who was the official Carmelite theologian. John was not a professional theologian, but he was well trained.

Friar John was an able student and might have been expected to pursue a university career after his ordination in 1567, but he was clearly more devoted to contemplative prayer than the classroom. For a time he considered leaving the Carmelites for the more austere contemplative life

---

[1] Bernard McGinn, Mysticism in the Golden Age of Spain (Chicago: 2017) p. 231-238.

of the Carthusians. Then came the first major turning point in his life – his meeting with Teresa of Avila. In early 1567, the Carmelite general John Baptist Rossi (Rubeo) approved Teresa's incipient reform of the order. Probably in September of the same year Teresa met John at Medina del Campo and convinced him to join the reform because of its stress on contemplative prayer. At this time, Friar John also took the new name by which he is known to history – John of the Cross (Juan de la Cruz). When he finished his theological studies in 1568, he spent several months with Teresa to learn how to live the reformed style of Carmelite life. On November 28, John and another friar established the first male house of the reform at Duruelo, thus making John the founder of the male branch of the Reformed (Discalced) Carmelites.

John took a leading role in the spread of the reform, both as founder of houses, as spiritual director of the reformed nuns, and as rector of the new college for the Discalced at Alcalá de Henares in 1571. In May of 1572 Teresa asked John to help her as a confessor at the convent of the Encarnación in Avila (an unreformed house) to which she had been recalled as prioress. Thus, for some years (1572-77) the two worked together and doubtless had much discussion on the nature of mystical prayer and union. Teresa, although not above poking fun at the serious John from time to time, consistently testified to his sanctity and spiritual wisdom. In a letter to Mother Ana de Jesús, who was having doubts about John's capacities, dated November 1578, she says:

> I was amused, daughter, of how groundless is your complaining, for you have in your very midst my father (mi padre), John of the Cross, a heavenly and divine man. I tell you daughter, from the time he left and went down there I have not found anyone in Castile like him, or anyone who communicates so much fervor in walking along the way of heaven....I declare to you that I would be most happy to have my Fray John of the Cross here, who truly is the father of my soul and from whom it benefited most in its conversations with him.[2]

For Teresa, John had become a pillar of the reform and a skilled spiritual director.

[2] Letter 278:1-2 in The Collected Letters of St. Teresa of Avila, translated by Kieran Kavanagh, 2 volumes (Washington D.C.: 2001).

All was not well, however, with the Spanish Carmelites. The tensions between the reformed and the unreformed camps of the order were growing and the internal dynamics of the order and its relation to the general in Rome were dysfunctional. The reforming camp went beyond their official mandate in some instances, and the unreformed group (originally favourable or indifferent) soon reacted in a strongly negative way – another sad chapter in the history of internal squabbles in religious orders. In January 1576, John was arrested by the unreformed (Observant) Carmelites but was soon released. He was arrested again and he was taken from Avila and brought to Toledo, where he was imprisoned in the monastery jail for nine months. This was a crisis for the reform movement, especially because the secrecy of his arrest left his friends in the dark about his whereabouts and health. Teresa of Avila penned a series of letters of complaints and petition, doing all in her power to free her friend. Challenging as it was, the imprisonment marked the second great turning point in the life of John the mystic. There was malice in his imprisonment. They hoped to hurt Teresa by hurting John. Teresa put great efforts into getting John released but to no avail. She petitioned the king and queen. It is noticeable that many of John's brothers did not put in the same effort.

The idea of monastic prisons seems strange today, but they were a part of medieval religious life for the correction of wayward priests and nuns who had chosen a consecrated life, who had betrayed it in some way, and whom the church would not allow to return to a secular state. John's Observant Carmelite captors were convinced that he was a dangerous renegade and therefore used the opportunity to treat him savagely. It was during these nine months of torture by supposed brothers that John learned the real cost of discipleship. The details of John's mistreatment comprised of imprisonment in a small cell with little light; wretched food; no change of clothes; constant harassment, especially about the failure of the reform; suffering from both cold and heat; savage beatings by the whole community once a week. In short, his treatment was totally inhuman. John testifies to the difficulty of the ordeal in the first of his surviving letters (1581), where he says to the nun Catalina de Jesús, "Be consoled with the thought that you are not as abandoned and alone as I am down here [at Baeza]. For after that whale swallowed me up and vomited me out on this alien port (Jonah 2:1-2), I have never merited to see her again [referring to Teresa of Avila] or the saints up there." John's reference to Jonah's three days in the belly of the whale (a type of Christ's death and resurrection) was an evocation of the transformation he experienced during his imprisonment, as the letter makes clear in what follows: "God has done well, for, after all, abandonment is a steel file and the endurance of darkness leads to great light. May it please God that we do not walk in darkness."[3]

By the summer of 1578, John was convinced he was dying and resolved to try to escape. Later accounts emphasise miraculous aspects of the story, especially the aid of the Blessed Virgin; but the event is remarkable enough in itself. On the night of August 15-16, John pried open his cell door, ripped up his sheets to serve as a rope and descended into an enclosed garden, having entrusted himself to a dangerous leap (a leap of faith!) to complete his descent. Eventually he got over the garden wall to reach safety. Near death with exhaustion, he showed up at the convent of reformed Carmelite nuns in Toledo, who hid him from his Observant pursuers until a friendly cleric spirited him out of the city to the protection of his brethren. Soon after his release, John began sharing his prison poetry with the reformed nuns and friars and explaining its meaning. A major mystical voice had been born. One of the most remarkable things about John's imprisonment is that being locked up seems to have unlocked his creativity. Although known as an excellent spiritual director during the first decade of his life in the reform (1567-77), he wrote little, save perhaps for a few letters that have not survived. Subsequent to his release he spent the next seven years producing more poems, a series of aphorisms, and four important prose commentaries.

John's spiritual counsel had been valued before his imprisonment, as we can see from the testimony of Teresa. Nevertheless, the interest the nuns and friars took in his poetry, his explanations of it, and his spiritual direction grew greatly in the following years. The nuns and friars who submitted testimonies about his sanctity dwell on the effect of his conversation.

The years following John's 1578 escape were busy. The reform movement of the Discalced was officially recognised by Gregory XIII in June of 1580. During the next decade John was elected to a number of leadership posts and was quite active, despite his lifelong commitment to solitude and silence. For the understanding of his mystical teaching it is important to

---

[3] John of the Cross, Letter 1 in Kavanagh, Rodriguez, Collected Works of Saint John of the Cross (Washington D.C.: 1991) p. 736.

consider the development of his writings during this time. As noted, John began sharing his prison poems with his brothers and sisters, especially the nuns of the convent of Beas, where he served as confessor and spiritual director in 1578 and 1579. It was in response to the questions of the nuns about the meaning of these poems that he first began writing commentaries, specifically what became the Ascent of Mount Carmel, dedicated to explaining the poem "En una noche oscura" ("On a dark night"), as well as the Spiritual Canticle, which commented on the "Canciones", the long poem beginning, "A donde te escondiste?" ("Where have you hidden...?"). John's prose works were an outgrowth of his vocation as a spiritual director. We also possess other, briefer witnesses to John's spiritual counsel, such as the four groups of *Sayings of Light and Love*, consisting of 175 aphorisms taken down by those he was advising.

Fray Juan Evangelista provides testimony about John's writing habits:

"I saw him write these books and I never saw him open a book in order to write them. He relied upon his communion with God, and it can be clearly seen that they are all the result of experience and practice and that he had personal experience of the subject of his writings."[4]

Both during his time as rector at the College at Baeza (1579-82) and after his transfer as prior to the convent at Granada (1582-85) John continued to work on the commentaries, revising and expanding both the base poem "A donde te escondiste?" by adding new stanzas and working on the prose explanation. In 1582 John met the pious widow Doña Ana del Mercado y Peñalosa, who soon became his penitent and friend. It was for her that he wrote the last of his mystical poems, "O llama de amor viva" ("O living flame of love"). At her request, he also wrote a commentary on the poem, probably at Granada in 1585. Juan Evangelista testifies that he composed it in two weeks. A second, slightly revised version of this commentary was his last work, produced in the final months of 1591.

The relation between John's three surviving prose works (counting the *Ascent/Night* as a single work) is complicated. Hans Urs von Balthasar,

---

[4] see Appendix A in E. Allison Peers, The Complete Works of John of the Cross, 3 vols., (London: 1935) 3:350, 352-53.

following Jean Baruzi, notes that each treatise "in its own way contains the whole on different levels that are not logically commensurable".[5] Thus, it is hard to decide how and in what order to read the corpus. The *Ascent of Mount Carmel* is the longest and most detailed work, but it deals primarily with the initial stages of the mystical path and John abandoned the book as its endless subdivisions became unworkable. The *Dark Night* is shorter and more coherent, but it too abandons commentary on the poem after a few stanzas and was not meant to be an account of the whole spiritual life. The *Spiritual Canticle* is John's meditation based on the Song of Songs. Finally, the late and short *Living Flame of Love*, dealing primarily with the goal of mystical union and transformation, has often been seen as John's masterpiece, although it describes mystical states that even the author admitted may seem incomprehensible to most people. This chapter will first consider, the Cross in John, the human person in his view, the *Ascent/Dark Night*, and follow with treatments of the *Canticle* and the *Living Flame*.

During these years of writing, John was busy furthering the reform. In 1585 he was elected vicar provincial for Andalusia, which meant that he had to travel extensively, founding seven new convents. In 1588 he was chosen as the first advisor for the new government of the Reformed Carmelites (called the Consulta) and therefore took up residence at Segovia. In June of 1590, however, the provincial Nicolás Doria (1539-1594) summoned a special chapter at Madrid in order to attack his foe, Jerónimo Gracian (1545-1614), the great friend of Teresa. John did not agree with Doria's action or with his attempts to change the rules regarding the nuns, and so he was relieved of his office in 1591. More disturbing was the effort of some of his enemies in the order to expel him from the Discalced. To someone who had suffered so much for his commitment to Teresa's vision this must have been a hard cross. Nonetheless, John took these events in his stride, welcoming the solitude he found in the small convent of La Peñuela and planning to go to Mexico as a missionary. It was not to be. In September he became ill with a foot infection and was transferred to Ubeda. Once again, John was badly treated by his brethren (this time reformed Carmelites). During these final months he experienced a second intense sharing in Christ's passion, both through his illness and painful medical treatments and through rejection by his fellow friars. According to the

---

[5] Hans Urs von Balthasar, "St. John of the Cross", in The Glory of the Lord: A Theological Aesthetics, vol. 3, Studies in Theological Style: Lay Styles (San Francisco: 1986) p. 169.

accounts we have, he remained patient and serene, preparing for death. During this time his gentleness softened the attitude of those who were hostile to him. On the night of December 13, John received the last rites. Fray Juan Evangelista reports, "On the night of his death he kept asking very anxiously what hour it was. When they told him it was eleven o'clock he said: 'Ah! At midnight we shall go and sing Matins in Heaven.'"[6] And so it was.

The Cross:

St. Paul speaks of coming to know Christ. He met the risen Christ on the road to Damascus (Acts 9:1-19). He came to know Christ and him crucified (see 1 Cor 1:17-25). "For God's foolishness is wiser than human wisdom and God's weakness is stronger than human strength" (1 Cor 1:25). In the letter to the Philippians he said:

> "...because of Christ I have come to consider all these advantages that I had as disadvantage. Not only that, but I believe nothing can happen that will outweigh the supreme advantage of knowing Christ Jesus my Lord. For him I have accepted the loss of everything, and I look on everything as so much rubbish if only I can have Christ, and be given a place in him. I am no longer trying for perfection by my own efforts, but I want the faith that comes through faith in Christ and is for God and based on faith. All I want is to know Christ and the power of his resurrection and to share his sufferings by reproducing the pattern of his death. That is how I hope to take my place in the resurrection of the dead."
>
> (Phil 3:7-12)

In this passage Paul describes his transformation in Christ and how he had to set aside what he held previously of most value. This is because he has come to know Christ. He describes how he has to know Christ and this is worth so much more. He has to know the surpassing greatness of Christ Jesus. "To know", in the Biblical sense, implies a deep, personal knowledge and relationship. Surpassing (*hyperechon* in Greek) is a strong word

---

[6] see Appendix A in E. Allison Peers, The Complete Works of John of the Cross: Doctor of the Church, 3 vols., (London: 1935) 3:334.

meaning excelling. He considers the past things as "refuse". The word Paul uses for refuse is *skybala* in Greek. This was a rude word in Paul's time and his audience would have blinked at the audacity of Paul's language. To gain Christ and enter into a profound communion with him makes Paul's leaving behind the things of the past. Paul wishes to recover the righteousness that comes from God. Righteousness has the sense of a proper relationship with God. He receives this righteousness through faith in Christ. To know Christ means to experience him as a life giving Spirit (see 1 Cor 15:45; 2 Cor 3:17). Christ's resurrection shows God's action and its meaning goes well beyond the restoration of his life. When God raised Jesus from the dead, a new power was unleashed in the world. He makes of us a new creation. He goes on to talk about sharing the sufferings. Paul wishes to unite his sufferings with Christ. Fellowship is a key term in the letter (see 1:5-7; 2:1; 4:14f) Paul describes in this part of the letter. He suffers in union with Christ and he comes to share in the resurrection. He goes on to say in this part of the letter that he is not perfect but he still grows in the faith and knowledge of Christ.

John of the Cross had a deep experience of the cross during his time of imprisonment. Twice a day the friars took him out and flogged him. They demanded he renounce Teresa and her reform. He declared himself to poverty of spirit. He now had no power and had nothing. When John was back in his cell he would hear his captors tell lies about Teresa and how her reform had failed totally. They would tell John all had forgotten him – he was totally alone. He could no longer feel God's presence. Whenever he tried to pray all he encountered was a cavernous emptiness. He would say in his poetry "Where have you hidden, my Beloved?" He called to mind the 'Song of Songs'. Now he began to write poetry. The poetry comprises the Dark Night, but he also wrote much of the Spiritual Canticle. He had passed with Christ from death to life.

Mirabai Starr who wrote on John of the Cross speaks of how when deep darkness enters our life: "You stop fighting and exhausted rest in the darkness of unknowing. You have been drained and shattered... You sit in your brokenness and listen to the sound of your own breathing."[7] Into the darkness comes a subtle inflow of sweetness. Here we meet Christ. This is

---

[7] Mirabai Starr (ed.), Saint John of the Cross: Devotion, Prayers and Living Wisdom (Boulder, Co.: 2012).

the journey John leads us on when all is dark. Starr is a daughter of the counter-culture of America. In 1972, Mirabai's mother and her younger brother and sister went on a long road trip and then the family embraced an alternative back to the land lifestyle. She was a very sensitive person and easily hurt. Her experiences of people abusing substances and other bad experiences hurt her deeply. She knew the dark night intimately.[8] As a teenager she lived at the Lama foundation, a community that honoured all the world's faiths. Mirabai became an adjunct professor of Philosophy and World Religions at the University of New Mexico. She lectures extensively on the themes of grief and loss. Her youngest daughter, Jenny, was killed in a road accident in 2001, at the age of fourteen. On that day, Mirabai's first book, a translation of John's Dark Night of the Soul, appeared. She looked at her experience as a dark night and she came to see the connection between profound loss and longing for God. When she speaks of John's dark night, she is speaking of her own experience of darkness.

John tells us to meditate on the person of Christ in our lives, especially when we have to face suffering and loss. The son took on human nature and elevated it into God's own beauty. He faced sorrow, anguish and death but these were transformed into new life. John says: "...in this elevation of all things through the incarnation of his Son and the glory of his resurrection according to the flesh, not only did the Father beautify creatures partially, but we can say, he clothed them entirely in beauty and dignity" (Canticle 5:4). The soul is led to seek deeper and come to know the incarnate Word until it reaches face-to-face vision in Heaven.

The important christological text in Ascent 2, 22 underlines the centrality and finality of the Word's coming in the flesh as the Father's ultimate message to humanity. Since the incarnation, John says, we should not seek any new messages, visions, or revelations from God but fix our eyes on Christ as "brother, companion, master, ransom, and reward" (Ascent 2, 22, 5). Because Christ redeemed the soul solely for his own sake, she now owes him a total response of love (Canticle 1, 1). As John insists in another key christological chapter (Ascent 2, 7), the path leading to eternal life is narrow. Although the path is a constricted one (Matt. 7:14), Jesus told us how it may be traversed when he preached the necessity of taking up one's

---

[8] see Mirabai Starr, Caravan of No Despair: A Memoir of Loss and Transformation (Sounds True, Colorado: 2015).

cross and following him (citing Mark 8:34-35 and many other texts). If we walk the road in nakedness and detachment, we will discover that "[t]he cross is a supporting staff and greatly lightens and eases the journey" (Ascent 2, 7, 7). John insists, "A person makes progress only by imitating Christ, who is the Way, the Truth, and the Life" (Ascent 2, 7, 8, citing John 14:6). This imitation must extend even to annihilation, because the journey of following Christ, "does not consist in consolations, delights, and spiritual feelings, but in the living death of the cross, sensory and spiritual, exterior and interior (Ascent 2:7.11). Although John sometimes talks about a general imitation of Christ in one's life (see Ascent 1:13,3-4), his fundamental concern is imitating Christ in bearing the cross. Truly devout people "seek the living image of Christ crucified within themselves, and thereby they are pleased rather to have something taken away from them and to be left with nothing (Ascent 3:35.5). The necessity of taking up the cross is a frequent theme in John's writings (Ascent 1:5.8, Canticle 3:5). As he succinctly put it in a fragmentary letter to Padre Luis de San Angelo, "Do not seek Christ without the cross" (Letter 24).

There is suffering in life. We cannot escape. John knew this but even in his darkest hour he followed Christ and in him was born to new life. He could speak of the Dark Night of the Soul, but in union with Christ he experienced a resurrection. He could also write the poetry of the 'Canticle'. In accepting our cross in union with Christ we are on a journey to new life and a life in union with God. When we surrender into the hands of the Father, in union with Jesus, our experiences of the cross then we find peace and become a new creation. This can be a slow but dynamic process. John of the Cross has explained to us the way to do this.

John's View of the Human Person:

John agrees with Gen 1:26 that the fundamental essence of human nature is its creation in God's image and likeness. Flowing from this John speaks of three forms of likeness or presence, or uniting with God. The first is the presence of similarity of essence by which God is found in all things, giving them life and being. The second similarity is "his presence by grace, in which he abides in the soul, pleased and satisfied with it". "The third is his presence by spiritual affection for God usually grants his presence to devout souls in many ways by which he refreshes, delights them" (Canticle 11:3).

Stanzas 20-21 of the Canticle are an address by the Bridegroom to the Bride picturing the world of nature and inviting her to be soothed and at rest. John speaks in his commentary on these verses of how spiritual transformation integrates and harmonises the powers of sense and spirit. "In these two stanzas the Bridegroom, the Son of God, gives the bride-soul possession of peace and tranquility by conforming the lower part to the higher, cleansing it of all its imperfections, bringing under rational control the natural faculties and natures and quieting all the other faculties" (Canticle 20/21,4).

Stanza 20 speaks of:

> "Swift-winged birds,
> lions, stags and leaping roes,
> mountains, lowlands and river banks,
> waters, winds, and ardors,
> watching fears of night."

John says these words refer to the disordered faculties of the soul and these are the parts of us that seek peace, the peace that comes from the Bridegroom. The swift-winged birds he identifies as the interior senses of fantasy and imagination. The soul also has two inclinations (appetites in John's vocabulary) – the irascible appetite, or inclination to avoid or resist what is offered to the soul (the lions) and the concupiscible appetite, the inclination to seek what is good and flee what is evil (the "stags" and "leaping roes"). In the 'Ascent of Mount Carmel' (1:11,1-4) John speaks of our over attachment to created things. John's treatment of how we overcome selfishness can seem severe and ruthless, but he has a goal in mind. He aims for a complete psycho-physical integration of the human person.[9] We are as human beings broken and confused. It is in love, the love of the Bridegroom, we accept ourselves and become more integrated. In the union of love in the Dark Night, John says: "God gathers together all the strengths, faculties and appetites of the soul, spiritual and sensory alike, so that the energy and power of this whole harmonious composite may be employed in this love" (Night 2:11,4).

---

[9] Steven Payne, John of the Cross and the Cognitive Value of Mysticism: An Analysis of Sanjuanist Teaching and its Philosophical Implications for Contemporary Discussions of Mystical Experience, New Syntheses Historical Library 37 (Dodrecht: 1990) p. 19.

The higher, spiritual parts of the soul John traditionally describes as threefold – the three faculties of intellect, memory and will. This is an idea he took from Augustine.[10] John says (in stanza 20) that the mountains, lowlands and river banks figure or represent the inordinate actions of these powers. Mountains are too high by inordinate excess, lowlands are acts that are low and defective, and the river banks are not totally level and thus signify some imperfection of intellect, memory or will (Canticle 20/21,8). Finally John reads the 'waters, winds, and ardors, watching fears of night' as natural passions or emotions: "The waters denote the emotions of sorrow...", "The winds allude to the emotions of hope...", "The ardors refer to the emotions of the passion of joy that inflame the heart like fire", "By the watching fears of night are understood the emotions of fear" (Canticle 20/21,9).

The intellect gains knowledge, while spiritual knowledge comes to it as a gift infused into the passive intellect. He says in the Ascent of Mount Carmel:

> It must be known, then, that the understanding can receive knowledge and intelligence by two channels: the one natural and the other supernatural. By the natural channel is meant all that the understanding can understand, whether by means of the bodily senses or by its own power. The supernatural channel is all that is given to the understanding over and above its natural ability and capacity.
>
> (Ascent 2:10,2)

He goes on to describe visions, revelations, locutions and spiritual feelings and the 'dark and general knowledge' that is gained in contemplation (Ascent 2:10,3-4).

The faculty of 'memory' in John may be called a faculty of attention or relation. It is an attention to recall past images and concepts that reside in the fantasy or in the soul itself in natural knowledge (e.g. Ascent 3:7,1). It can also refer to an attentive hope directed to the mystery of God in supernatural knowing (see Ascent 2). This faculty needs to be purified by the supernatural virtue of hope (Ascent 3:2-15). When we can hope and

---

[10] Augustine, De Trinitate, especially books 9-15.

believe, we gain strength. If we have hope then we can live with many things. Nietzsche said, "he who has a why can deal with any how". The idea of 'having a why' was fundamental for the development of Viktor Frankl's logotherapy.[11] Behind all our search for meaning is a search for God. John found his meaning in Jesus the Christ and his union with him. This enabled him to transform his prison experience.

The will is the spiritual faculty of the appetite and affectivity. It employs and coordinates all the affections and appetites, longings, pleasures, emotions and desires. It is the seat of love. "The intellect and the other faculties cannot admit or deny anything without the intervention of the will" (Ascent 3:34,1). John analyses the active purgation of the sensory appetites in Book 1 of the Ascent of Mount Carmel and he presents an account of the active purgation of the memory's natural and supernatural apprehensions in Ascent 3:11-15. He presents an unfinished analysis of the emotions of joy, hope, sorrow and fear in Ascent 3:16-42. His intention is to show us how we must empty ourselves of all voluntary appetites, desires and emotions, if we are to receive the grace of charity, the "dark and obscure love" (Flame 3:49), paralleling the "dark knowledge" of faith that gives access to the infinite God and in union with him a true love for all created things. He expresses this in a letter (Letter 14 in the Collected Works) sent to a fellow Carmelite around 1589. John says:

> It is worth knowing, then, that the appetite is the mouth of the will. It is opened wide when it is not encumbered or occupied with any mouthful of pleasure. When the appetite is centered on something, it becomes narrow by this very fact, since outside God everything is narrow. That the soul have success in journeying to God and being joined to him, it must have the mouth of its will opened only to God himself, empty and dispossessed of every morsel of appetite, so that God may fill it with his love and sweetness; and it must remain with this hunger and thirst for God alone, without desiring to be satisfied by any other thing, since here below it cannot enjoy God as he is in himself.

[11] Viktor Frankl, Man's Search for Meaning (New York: 1985) see also, The Unconscious God (New York: 1985).

Transformation takes place by giving up the possession of created things, which can never fulfill of themselves the infinite desires of the soul. It is when we come close to God that integration takes place.

When we discover we are loved, we can love in return. The soul falls in love with all people, all things. This is because it knows the love of God which is past understanding (Eph 3:9) and experiences this love by the power of the Holy Spirit. John says:

> Corresponding to the exquisite quality with which the intellect receives divine wisdom, being made one with God's intellect, is the quality with which the soul gives this wisdom, for it cannot give it save according to the mode in which it was given. And corresponding to the exquisite quality by which the will is united to goodness is the quality by which the soul gives in God the same goodness to God.... And, no more no less, according to the exquisite quality by which it knows the grandeur of God, being united to it, the soul shines and diffuses the warmth of love.
>
> (Flame 3:78)

The substance of the soul, according to John, is the place of permanent union with God at the height of the mystical path. Speaking of the drink of union that 'deifies, elevates and immerses' the soul, John says:

> For even though the soul is always in this sublime state of spiritual marriage once God has placed her in it, the faculties are not always in actual union although the substance is. Yet in this substantial union [unión sustancial] the faculties are frequently united too; and they drink in this inner wine cellar, the intellect understanding, the will loving, and so on.
>
> (Canticle 26:11)

For John the soul's centre is God (Flame 1:12). The depths of the soul are called by John the "profound caverns of feeling, the infinite capacity of the soul to receive the 'divine substantial touches and words' that give direct access to God". Stanza three of the Living Flame of Love describes the soul's contact with God in the following words:

"Oh, lamps of fire
In whose splendours
the deep caverns of feeling,
once obscure and blind,
now give forth, so rarely, so exquisitely,
both warmth and light to the Beloved."

When the caverns are purged and emptied of all things, one experiences an overwhelming and painful thirst for God and then God sends his touches and wounds love deep in the soul, as the most profound satisfaction and delight (Flame 3:19-23). "Thus it seems that the more the soul desires God the more it possesses him, and the possession of God delights and satisfies it..." (Flame 3:23). The flame of Love, the Holy Spirit, touches the soul at its deepest level. While in this life the soul is capable of going deeper and deeper through love into various centers until it reaches the deepest centre. "The soul's centre is God" (Flame 1:12). John says: "...God's love has arrived at wounding the soul in its ultimate and deepest centre, which is to illuminate it and transform it in its whole being, power and strength, and according to its capacity, until it appears to be God" (Flame 1:13). "While this is not as great as the union to be enjoyed in heaven" (Flame 1:28).

John tells us of the attitude we should have when entering the dark nights, both active and passive. This is the beginning of our journey, our ascent of Mount Carmel. John counsels us that to overcome both the sensory and the spiritual barriers to union with God it is necessary that

To reach satisfaction in all (todo} / desire satisfaction in nothing (nada).
To come to possess all / desire the possession of nothing.
To arrive at being all / desire to be nothing.
To come to the knowledge of all / desire the knowledge of nothing.

He then adds:

To come to taste what you have not / you must go by a way where you taste not.
To come to the knowledge you have not / you must go by the way you know not.

To come to the possession you have not / you must go by the way you possess not.
To come to be what you are not / you must go by the way in which you are not.

John concludes with the following summary of the dialectic of todo / nada:

When you delay over something [i.e., anything created] / you cease to rush towards the all [al todo]. To go from the all to the all / you must deny yourself of all in all [del todo al todo]. And when you come to the possession of the all / you must possess it without wanting anything, / because if you desire to have anything in having all, / you do not hold your treasure purely in God.

(Ascent 1:12.6-13)

John plays on the idea of nothing (nada) so that we can come to possess all (todo) in God and in union with him. An investigation of the Dark Night and the Ascent will help us see how John developed these ideas. God is the all (todo), the goal of human life. "Attachments to God and an attachment to creatures are contraries; there cannot exist in the same will a voluntary attachment to creatures and an attachment to God" (Ascent 1:6,1). This echoes the teaching of Jesus who said "where your treasure is, there will your heart be also" (Matt 6:21). At the end of the journey when we come to share the perfect love of God we can love all creatures and people in God. Among the exercises that were essential for John is silence. The root for silence is in the very nature of God. "The Father spoke one word, which was his Son, and this word he speaks always in eternal silence, and in silence must be heard in the soul" (No. 100 of Sayings of Light and Love). In letter 8 to the Carmelite nuns at Beas he says:

"There is no better remedy than to suffer, to do and be silent, and to close the senses through the inclination toward and practice of solitude and forgetfulness of ourselves ... it is impossible to advance without doing and suffering virtuously, all enveloped in silence."

John's prison experience informed his teaching and poetry. He draws on his experience to speak of the dark night.

The Dark Night:

The worst part of the ordeal John experienced was the feeling of the loss of God. Many years later John would write of the experience of desolation that formed the dark night. He spoke of the person who suffers the dark night as being "like one who is imprisoned in a dark dungeon, bound hand and foot, unable to see or feel any favour from heaven and earth" (2N 7:3). These words throw light on John's inner journey when he was a prisoner in a dark, small room and all the world seemed to be against him. He was truly alone.

In the Living Flame of Love, he describes this feeling of aloneness:

"...a person suffers great deprivation and feels heavy afflictions in the spirit that ordinarily overflow into the senses, for this flame is extremely oppressive. In this preparatory purgation the flame is not bright for a person, but dark.... It is not gentle, but afflictive. Even though it sometimes imparts the warmth of love, it does so with great torment and pain. And it is not delightful,... but it is consuming and contentious, making a person faint and suffer with self-knowledge... A person suffers from sharp trials in the intellect, severe dryness and distress in the will, and from the burdensome knowledge of their own miseries in the memory... In the substance of the soul they suffer abandonment, supreme poverty, dryness, cold.... They find relief in nothing, nor does any thought console them, so oppressed are they by this flame.... it truly seems to the soul that God has become displeased with it and cruel."

(Living Flame, 1:19-20)

John saw himself as being in communion with the lonely Christ in Gethsemane (Mk 14:32-42). Even in this desolation God's Spirit, the living flame of love, is active bringing new life, a new dawn of the Spirit. John experienced both the dark night and the new dawn of faith in his prison experience. He stresses that it is important we remember God is not absent in the dark nights; we take his silence to mean absence. John teaches us that even in the darkest hour we are not alone. John J. Murphy says: "God's presence is only realised with the recognition of God's absence. In this way, the concept of an infinite God is mediated in and through the limitations of a finite world".[12]

Iain Matthew points out that the nights that John speaks of, are the process of growth in prayer that involves three components: first an inflow of God, God entering the soul; the second, darkness – that is with the accent on bewildered suffering; and third "a creative response – faith, acceptance".[13]

Recollection begins in the active night of the spirit as the three faculties of memory, intellect and will are gradually instilled. As John summarised in the 'Sayings of Light and Love': "The humble are those who hide in their nothingness and know how to abandon themselves to God" (No. 163).

John speaks of how we are led from meditation to contemplation.[14] "The first sign is that just as the soul does not find satisfaction in the things of God it does not find it in anything created either". This means one feels dry night across the board. The soul feels no consolation anywhere. They feel surrounded by a strange sense of a total loss of satisfaction. "The second sign for the discernment of this purgation is that the memory ordinarily turns to God with solicitude and with painful care, thinking it is not serving God but backsliding, because it experiences the inability to derive satisfaction from the things of God". The soul becomes anxious and full of anxious questions. The mysterious world of faith in which it is now plunged makes the soul feel as if he or she were wasting their time. The soul experiences loss of meaningfulness, regarding its value system, its enthusiasm and its spiritual gusto. The soul feels it is bankrupt. There is the fear that somehow one is being punished. The person can come to realise that there are parts of us that are not right. We can know that we really are sinners and do hurt one another, ourselves and God. In the dark night God removes the defence mechanisms we built around ourselves. We become aware of our lack of sincerity.

---

[12] John J. Murphy, St. John of the Cross and the Philosophy of Religion: Love of Godand the Conceptual Parameters of a Mystical Experience, Mystics Quarterly 22 (1996), p. 163-86, cit 169.

[13] Iain Matthew, The Impact of God: Soundings from St. John of the Cross (London: 2010), p. 72ff.

[14] see 1 Night, 1:9. I am indebted to the work, Francis Kelly Nemeck, OMI, and Marie Theresa Coombs, Contemplation (Collegeville, MN: 1982) pg. 53-60, and 76-85.

"The third sign for the discernment of this purgation of the sense is the powerlessness, in spite of one's efforts, to meditate or to make use of the imagination as was one's previous custom.."

Contemplation at the beginning is dark and dry to the senses. Side by side with the inability to meditate is the fact that one is drawn to solitude... gradually in solitude we find peace.

John of the Cross, on the basis of his own experience or from his experience as a spiritual disaster, speaks of three 'spirits' that try to keep the pray-er from entering contemplation (see 1 Night 14:1-6). The first trial of the night of sense occurs when "the angel of Satan, which is the spirit of fornication, is given to them in order to buffet their senses with abominable and strong temptations and to afflict them with foul thoughts and very vivid images. This is sometimes a worse affliction for them than death."

The spirit fills the soul with wild fantasies and images. The term 'spirit of fornication' is found in Hosea 4:12; 5:4. John also borrows the phrase from St. Paul in 2 Cor 12:7 where Paul speaks of the thorn in the flesh that was sent to buffet him. Paul rebelled against the thorn but he was told in prayer "My grace is sufficient for thee" (2 Cor 12:9). The soul has to wait in patience.

Another spirit is the spirit of blasphemy. "At other times the spirit of blasphemy is added. It mingles blasphemy with all their ideas and thoughts. At times they are so forcefully suggested to the imagination that it almost makes these souls pronounce them. This causes great torment".

The soul blames everybody and sees everybody in a bad light and especially even themselves. This spirit arises from a deep-rooted selfishness as is the spirit of fornication in the soul. The soul craves to be in control – now all seems lost and one feels out of control.

"At still other times another abominable spirit which Isaiah calls 'spiritus vertiginis' (Isa 19:14) [the spirit of dizziness] is given to them, not for their downfall but to exercise them. The spirit darkens their senses in such a way that it fills them with a thousand scruples and perplexities, so intricate to their judgement that they can never satisfy themselves with anything, or find support for their judgement in any advice or idea."

The soul reels in a whirlwind of uncertainty. Intense spiritual anxiety grips the soul, loading it with thoughts that it is not serving God, and that God could not possibly love this soul. The soul listens to advice but in its confusion it cannot process what it is being told. Ignatius of Loyola (+1556) was a soldier firstly but was injured at the battle of Pamploma. His conversion began when he read a life of Christ and the lives of saints. He felt called to follow Christ. He became a pilgrim searching for God. Given his devotion to Mary, he went to the shrine of Our Lady in Montserrat in Catalonia. He went to a nearby town called Manresa. When St. Ignatius of Loyola was in Manresa trying to discern his vocation he was afflicted with doubt about whether he could live the life he was called to (Acta Patris Ignatii 20). He suffered severe mood swings (Acta 22-23) and even contemplated suicide (Acta 24). He surrendered in the face of these temptations to divine grace. He used his experience to form his teaching about the discernment of spirits which formed part of his spiritual exercises. His overcoming of the spirit of dizziness led him to contemplation. The spirit arises from another form of selfishness, the insatiable need for reassurance and the craving to know and understand. When we learn to surrender, to practice abandonment of all things into the hands of God we are led to his peace and a new understanding.

In the end "contemplation is nothing but a hidden, peaceful, loving inflow of God. If it is given room it will inflame the spirit with love" (Ascent 1:13,11). John described the Night that leads to this dawn as an experience of Hell:– "Sometimes this experience [the night] is so vivid that it seems to the soul that it sees Hell and perdition open before it. They are the ones who go down into Hell alive" (2N 6:6). "…In truth the soul experiences the sorrows of Hell, all of which reflect the feeling of God's absence, of being chastised and rejected by him… The soul experiences this and even more for it seems that this affliction will last forever" (2 N 6:2-3 and 2N 7:4).

To give us courage John uses another image, this time of fire on wood. He calls the Holy Spirit the 'Living Flame of Love'. He now uses the analogy of wood on the fire. He speaks of the fire burning the wood: "Its effect is like that of fire on wood. First the fire blackens the wood, causes it to sweat and this envelopes it with smoke, but then when it has been purified in this way, the wood is burnt through from within and transformed into fire" (Flame 1:19-21; 2N 10:1-4; Canticle 38). We are the wood. When we feel the flame of the Spirit we find all kinds of selfishness and imperfections in ourselves, but as we grow we become one with the flame of love. We become fire, that is, we are alive in the Spirit. Thérèse of Lisieux (+1897) read John of the Cross. She did not read many books but she made an exception for John of the Cross. From him she learnt the importance of abandonment (in French abandon). She surrendered all things, especially her littleness, into the hands of God, allowing him to pray through her. Through her surrender many have come to find peace, inspired by St. Thérèse.

The Divine Canticle:

John's spiritual canticle is, if you like, the view from the top of the mountain. It catches in a global sense John's project in writing. It is written from the view of one who now lives in union with God. It is all the more startling to realise that John composed most of his poem while in prison in Toledo. It marks John's reflection on the Song of Songs. The shape of the poem follows the traditional pattern of purification, illumination and union.[15]

He begins with verses 1-12, which are the start of the journey:

> "Where have you hidden,
> Beloved and left me mourning.
> You fled like a stag
> after wounding me"
>
> (Stanza 1, Canticle)

Isa 45:15 says: "Truly, You are a God who is hidden." John tells us in 1:11 that it is by love and faith that we can seek him and he reveals himself to us. "The hiding place of the Word, as John asserts, is the bosom of the Father, that is, the divine essence" (Canticle 1:3). Later he says "You do very well, O soul, to seek him ever as one hidden, for you exalt God and

---

[13] see Antonio Maria Sicari, Il "Divino Cantico" (Foligno: 2011).

approach him higher and deeper than everything you can reach" (Canticle 1:12).

There is an interplay of voices between the soul, the bride and the bridegroom. In the first stanza the bride seeks the bridegroom. The whole canticle is like a wedding song. The bride speaks in thirty-two stanzas, the bridegroom speaks in seven stanzas (13, 20-23, 34-35) and the voices of others in stanza 5. The poem presents an ongoing dynamic of desire and eager searching leading to an encounter and union, one that catches the elusive presence and absence of the divine lover. In stanza 1 the bride yearns for the absent lover. She has experienced the wound of love and this has caused her to go away from all creatures and seek the beloved. In the Song of Songs the bride compares the bridegroom "to a stag and the mountain goat: My beloved is like a gazelle or a young stag (Song 2:9), she makes the comparison not only because he is withdrawn and solitary and flees from companions like the stag, but also because of the swiftness with which he shows and then hides himself" (Canticle 1:15).

> The bride continues:
> Shepherds, you who go
> up through the sheep-folds to the hill,
> if by chance you see
> him I love most,
> tell him I am sick, I suffer and
> I die."
>
> (Stanza 2)

The bride seeks the comfort of those who can tell her where her lover is. "Her desires, affections and moanings 'are called shepherds" because they pasture the soul with spiritual goods" (Canticle 2:2). Her desire spurs her to seek God.

"The soul is aware that neither her sighs and prayers nor the help of good intermediaries, about which she speaks in the first and second stanzas, are sufficient for her to find her beloved" (Canticle 3:1). Nothing can satisfy the bride only full union with the bridegroom. John here catches the idea of desire and longing that characterise the seeking of God, the search for love.

Stanza 3 reads:

138

"Seeking my love,
I will head for the mountains and the watersides,
I will not gather flowers,
nor fear wild beasts;
I will go beyond strong men and frontiers."

(Stanza 3)

She dedicates all her energy here to seeking the Beloved. The soul must do everything in its power to find God, ever mindful of the words of the Beloved "Seek and you shall find (Lk 11:9)" (Canticle 3:2).

Stanzas 8 and 9 read:

"How do you endure
O life, not living where you live,
and being brought near death
by the arrows you receive
from that which you conceive of your Beloved?

Why, since you wounded
this heart, don't you heal it?
And why, since you stole it from me,
do you leave it so,
and fail to carry off what you have stolen?"

(Stanzas 8 and 9)

The soul wishes to live in the love of the one who loves it (Canticle 8:3). The soul has been wounded by love and desire and now dedicates itself to finding and living in this love. Jesus represented the life of the soul. He said "I am the resurrection and the life... whoever believes in me will never die" (Jn 11:25), "I am the way, the truth and the life" (Jn 14:6), and "I am the bread of life..." (Jn 6:35,48). Saint Paul says: "...it is no longer I that live but Christ lives in me: The life I now live in the body, I live by faith in the Son of God, who loved me and gave himself for me" (Gal 2:20). "... your life is now hidden with Christ in God" (Col 3:3).

The Canticle began with the soul's self knowledge and this formed an impetus for seeking God. The soul sought God in creation (Stanzas 4-6). Then the narrative shifted to seeking the one who wounded the soul with love. The wounded stag stands for the Divine lover. The final stanzas of the stage of purification are when the bride-soul asks the Bridegroom to "reveal his presence" and slay her with love, because love's sickness cannot be cured in any other way (11:2). The sickness of love is both presence and absence. Some glimpses of the beauty of God increase the fervor and the desire to see God. "The love of God is the soul's health, and the soul does not have full health until love is complete [in Heaven] (11:11). It is in God that all our different energies are integrated. He gives us meaning and peace. In this way the love of God heals us and is our health.

> "For the sickness of love
> is not cured except by your
> very presence and image."
>
> (Stanza 11)

The bride calls her love "love-sickness" because as yet the soul is feeble in love (11:13).

Stanza 12 returns to the theme of faith, comparing enlightened faith with a 'crystalline font' which provides a reflection of the Beloved.

> "O spring like crystal,
> If only, on your silvered-over faces
> You would suddenly form
> the eyes I have desired
> which I bear sketched deep within my heart."
>
> (Stanza 12)

Faith is like a spring of water nourishing the soul (Jn 4:14 and 7:39 are cited) and also a crystal because its truths are clear and certain. The substance of faith will have the colour of gold when we come to know God (12:3-4). In this life we live by hope-filled faith and love (12:6). The soul and the beloved become one in the transformation of love (12:7).

Stanzas 13 – 19 deal with the second stage in the spiritual life, the stage of illumination. The illuminative stage involves intense purification and in some cases the beginning of mystical gifts such as rapture. It is also the phase of spiritual betrothal. Introducing stanza 13 John says: "The reason the soul suffers so intensely for God at this time is that she is drawing nearer to him: so she has greater experience within herself of the void of God, of the very heavy darkness, and the spiritual fire that dries up and purges her so that she may be united to him" (13:1). The void John speaks of is now that the soul is empty of attachments and waits for God to enter. Stanza 13 speaks where God withdraws experiences of his presence because these states are too powerful for the soul.

"Withdraw then, Beloved,
I am taking flight!
Bridegroom: Return, dove,
the wounded stag
is in sight on the hill,
cooled by the breeze of your flight."

(Stanza 13)

The stag representing the Bridegroom is now revealed as wounded in his reciprocal love for the soul. "Among lovers the wound of one is a wound for both, and the two have but one feeling" (13:9). As much as we seek God he seeks us all the more. He loves the soul deeply. Both seek to love each other with an infinite love.

Stanzas 14 and 15 are treated together by John. The dove's spiritual flight is seen as "a high state and union of love… called spiritual betrothal with the Word, the son of God (14/15, Introduction 2). He speaks about the peaceful love between the Bride and her Lover, the soul and Jesus. Purification is not yet complete. John speaks of the delights the soul enjoys (14/15:4). The soul can now say with St. Francis of Assisi: "My God and my all" (14/15: 6-15). The last line of the stanza reads:

"The whistling of love-stirring breezes"

This refers to the touches of love received deep in the Spirit. Saint Francis, when he began his life of prayer, was enraptured with this love and he spent hours lost in contemplating this great love, "the love that is better than life" (Ps 63:3).

"The tranquil night,
at the time of the rising dawn,
silent music,

sounding solitude,
the supper that refreshes, and deepens love."
(Stanza 15)

John here is speaking of the dawn that comes after the experience of the night (14/15, 22-23). Here contemplation is compared to the "lonely sparrow" of Ps 102:7 (14/15, 24). John uses the paradoxical idea of 'silent music'. This is the peaceful way in which the Creator is seen in creation and is closely related to the 'sounding solitude' of God's presence (14/15, 22-27). John speaks of the 'supper that refreshes and deepens love' which is nothing other than the Bridegroom himself. This expression also has eucharistic overtones. "These words declare the effect of the divine union of the soul with God in which God's very own goods are graciously and bounteously shared in common with the bride, the soul. He himself is for her the supper that refreshes and deepens love" (14/15, 29).

In verses 16-18, John speaks of the three opponents to this higher prayer. The first enemy is the little foxes (Song of Songs 2:15) which are the images that rise up in the imagination to disturb the quiet rest of the spiritual part (16:2-5). The second opponent, figured in the 'deadening north wind' of stanza 17 is the spiritual dryness that hampers interior satisfaction (17:2-3). To counter this the soul asks the south-wind, the Holy Spirit, (John cites Song of Songs 4:16) to awaken love in her. The third obstacle is "the nymphs of Judaea" (see Song of Songs 2:7, 5:8, 8:4). These are the imaginations, fantasies, movements and affections of the lower part of the soul (18:3-4, 8). These pass through the grace of the Holy Spirit. Once we know what is going on, anxiety is removed and we can abandon all into the hands of God, whom we now know loves us (Thérèse).

Stanza 19 ends the ascent of the illuminative stage and prepares us for the discussion of the life of union with God (stanzas 20-35). Here the bride asks for different gifts from the Beloved, that he communicate himself inwardly in the superior part of the soul, that he inform her faculties with the glory of his divinity, that the communication be indescribable as was Paul's experience when he was lifted to the third heaven (2 Cor 12:2) and that he would come to love the virtues he has given her. John says that the soul wishes to experience "the essential communication of the divinity to the soul" (19:4).

Bridegroom
 Swift-winged birds,
 lions, stags, and leaping roes,
 mountains, lowlands, and river banks,
 waters, winds, and ardors,
 watching fears of the night:

 By the pleasant lyres
 and the siren's song, I conjure you
 to cease your anger
 and not touch the wall,
 that the bride may sleep in deeper peace.
(Stanza 19)

In the Canticle and the Living Flame of Love John speaks about the spiritual marriage. In the last section of the Canticle and the Flame he puts emphasis on the Bible, especially the Song of Songs and the Psalms. John uses these to help us understand union and the transformation in love of the purified soul.

Stanzas 20/21 and 22 summarise the meaning of the spiritual marriage. Here the Divine Lover finally unites the higher and lower dimensions of the soul. John is now describing deep union and the bride can now only rejoice in the possession of the Beloved (20/21, 4-12). He uses verses from the Song of Songs (3:5, 5:1, 6:1-2) to illustrate spiritual marriage. Stanza 22 advances this general description with an account of the spiritual marriage as comprising union with God, deification that is participation of the divine nature (2 Peter 1:4) as well as transformation into God. He says: "The spiritual marriage is incomparably greater than the spiritual betrothal for it is a total transformation in the Beloved, in which each surrenders the entire possession of self to the other with a certain consummation of the union of love (Canticle 22:3)

 "The bride has entered
 the sweet garden of her desire,
 and she rests in delight,
 laying her neck
 on the gentle arms of her Beloved."
(Stanza 22)

143

She enters the "full delight of the state of spiritual marriage; now that she has also invoked and obtained the breeze of the Holy Spirit which entails the proper preparation and instrument for the perfection of this state" (22:2).

The next five stanzas (22-27) describe the gifts that the soul receives in spiritual marriage. The touches of love between the soul and the bridegroom shower graces on the soul. Stanza 23 takes as its theme the divine secrets that the Bridegroom communicates to the Bride:

"Beneath the apple tree:
there I took you for my own,
there I offered you my hand,
and restored you,
where your mother was corrupted.'
(Stanza 23)

Here John refers to Song of Songs 8:5. Just as Eve was corrupted in the garden, so Christ has redeemed us by the cross and gradually reveals to us the mysteries of the incarnation and the cross.

In Stanza 24 John takes up the image of the "little flowery bed" of the Song of Songs (Song 1:5). This represents the Bridegroom himself. With him the soul rests in peace. Here the bride experiences the joy of union (24:3-5), her perfect virtues (24:4-6) and the greatest gift of all, love (24:7). Now she experiences the perfect love that casts out fear (24:8). The conversation with the Song of Songs continues in Stanza 25:

"Following your footprints
maidens run along the way;
the touch of a spark,
the spiced wine,
cause flowings in them from the balsam of God."
(Stanza 25)

Here the bride rejoices in the gifts the Bridegroom has given the other souls. The "touch of a spark", which John connects with the Song of Songs 5:1 (My beloved put his head through the opening and my heart trembled at his touch) is the subtle touch the Beloved produces in the soul to inflame her with love (25:5-6). The spiced wine (Song 8:2) leads to a lengthy treatment (25:7-11) of the theme of mystical "inebriation" – "this is the intoxication the soul experiences in the love of the Holy Spirit, which lasts much longer than a transient spark" (27:8). Finally the "flowings from the balsam of God" are the acts of divine love that produce these effects in the soul (see Song 1:2).

In Stanza 26 John continues his idea of drinking of the love of God. Here in this union of love, substantial union is permanent since God has introduced the soul into the state of marriage (26:11). The soul wanders in the world but now the soul is in union with God (26:13). The absorption in love wipes the soul's slate clean (26:17). Despite the height of this wonderful state, there always remain imperfections in us as long as we are in this life (26:18-19).

Stanza 27 concludes the treatment of the gifts of the Bridegroom. Here John speaks of God both as Father and mother:

> "There he gave me his breast;
> there he taught me a sweet and living
> knowledge;
> and I gave myself to him,
> keeping nothing back;
> there I promised to be his bride."

Here the Lover God "himself becomes subject to her for her exaltation, as though he were her servant and she his lord" (27:1). Here we have perfect love between the two.

Stanzas 28-34 elucidate further characteristics of this loving union. John treats the spiritual marriage using the imagery of a gem or a jewel. He speaks of the perfect love that now exists between the Bride and the Bridegroom... "for the property of love is to make the lover equal to the object loved" (28:1). John says that the soul possessed of the Spirit of love glories "in holding that she has achieved this work in praise of her Beloved and lost all things of the world" (29:7).

The final stanzas of the Spiritual Canticle deal with the goal of union, the enjoyment of God in the eternal bliss of Heaven. The delights of final and perfect union begin already in this life. Stanza 36 is a kind of summary of the mutual love of the Bride and Bridegrrom:

"Let us rejoice, Beloved,
and let us go forth to behold ourselves in your beauty
to the mountain and to the hill,
to where the pure water flows,
and further, deep into the thicket."

(Stanza 36)

The love the soul experiences must overflow into our way of living (36:4). The soul becomes beautiful in God "my beauty will be your beauty and your beauty my beauty" (36:5). The Bride also wishes to unite her sufferings with the sufferings of the Bridegroom, Christ. This explains "deep into the thicket". Thérèse of Lisieux entered a long night of suffering in the last eighteen months of her life. She shared in Jesus' work of saving all people. John summarises his thought here:

"Oh! If we could but now fully understand how a soul cannot reach the thicket and wisdom of the riches of God, which are of many kinds, without entering the thicket of many kinds of suffering, finding in this her delight and consolation.... The gate entering into these riches of his wisdom [Eph. 3:13, 17-19 is cited] is the cross, which is narrow, and few desire to enter by it, but many desire the delights obtained from entering there."

(36:3)

Thérèse of Lisieux was united to God. She practiced her prayer of abandonment, of surrender into God's hands. She was given great sufferings but she remained faithful in this time of trial and she became a symbol of hope for many souls. She was known as "the healer of the 20th century". Her love went beyond the walls of the Carmel in Lisieux.

John shows us the view from the mountain top. Yet there are so many who are afraid and confused. Ingmar Bergman (+2007) made a film called "Wild Strawberries" (1967). In this sad film the main character Isak Borg, the lonely old professor reads this poem, when asked to resolve a debate on the existence of God. The poem was an 1819 Swedish hymn by Josef Wallin,

"Where is that friend, whom everywhere I seek?
When the day dawns, my longing only grows;
When the day flees, I still cannot find Him
Though my heart burns.

I see his traces, wherever power moves,
a flower blooms, or a leaf bends.
In the breath I draw, the air I breathe
His love is mixed."

Isak recites this poem in a nostalgic way. He wishes to find his lost friend but now feels he can't. He is lonely. The lives of John, Teresa and Thérèse point us to another reality. The sense of loss can just be the beginning of our search for God and in this search we find God is searching for us. It is in abandonment and prayer that we come to find God. John is our teacher and Thérèse, our little sister, who prays for us. They show us the way because they have been there before us.

The Living Flame of Love, The Holy Spirit:

The Greek word, *pneuma*, and the Hebrew word *ruach*, which are translated as spirit, mean both wind and breath. They refer to the dynamic movement and energy of air. The wind as a force can cause others to move. The words also refer to the breath of air that we use when we are talking. In Isaiah II we speak of the spirit resting on the person. The Spirit is the creator of new things. He is the Lord and the giver of life. He lives in us and by his gift the Father and Son live in us (Jn 14:16-23). In Paul's letter to the Romans we read: "...the Spirit helps us in our weakness. We do not know what we ought to pray for, but the Spirit himself intercedes for us through wordless groans" (Romans 8:26).

John has a rich teaching on the Holy Spirit. The idea of energy, new creation and the Spirit being the bond of love between the Father and the Son. The Holy Spirit is dynamic and transforms the lover into the beloved. He is fire.

The 'Living Flame of Love' is about how we are transformed by the power of the Holy Spirit.

1   O living flame of love
       that tenderly wounds my soul
       in its deepest center! Since
       now you are not oppressive,
       now consummate! if it be your will:
       tear through the veil of this sweet encounter!

2   O sweet cautery,
       O delightful wound!
       O gentle hand! O delicate touch that tastes of eternal life
       and pays every debt!
       in killing you changed death to life.

3   O lamps of fire!
       in whose splendors
       the deep caverns of feeling,
       once obscure and blind,
       now give forth, so rarely, so exquisitely, both warmth and light
       to their Beloved.

4   How gently and lovingly
       you wake in my heart,
       where in secret you dwell alone;
       and in your sweet breathing,
       filled with good and glory,
       how tenderly you swell my heart with love.

The flame is a flame of the divine life. It wounds the soul with the tenderness of God's love. The flame fulfills what the bride said in the Song of Songs: "As soon as he spoke my heart melted" (Song 5:6). For God's speech is the effect he produces in the soul (Flame 1:7). The soul's centre is God (Flame 1:12) and love is the inclination, strength and power for the soul making its way to God (Flame 1:13).

> "When the soul asserts that the flame of love wounds it in its deepest centre, it means that insofar as this flame reaches its substance, power and strength, the Holy Spirit assails and wounds it."
>
> (Flame 1:14)

In the Canticle (Stanza 38) John speaks of the action of the Spirit:

"There you will show me
what my soul has been seeking,
and then you will give me,
you, my life, will give me there
what you gave me on that other day"

There the bride wishes to share in God's love. The Spirit is God's love in person and introduces the bride into God's love. The bride came to know the Father and the Son by sharing in their love.

Stanza 39 says:

"The breathing of the air,
the song of the sweet nightingale,
the grove and its living beauty
in the serene night,
with a flame that is consuming and painless."

In this stanza she speaks of the breath or spiration of the Holy Spirit from God to her and from her to God (Canticle 39:2). This is the breathing of love. By his divine breath-like spiration, the Holy Spirit elevates the soul sublimely and informs her and makes her capable of breathing in God the same spiration of love that the Father breathes in the Son and the Son in the Father. This spiration of love is the Holy Spirit himself, who in the Father and the Son breathe out to her in this transformation in order to unite her with himself (Canticle 39:3). This is the same Spirit St. Paul speaks of: "Since you are children of God, God sent the Spirit of his Son into your hearts, calling to the Father (Gal 4:6). John here speaks of perfect love as being a flame. "It must consummate and transform the soul in God, and the inflammation and transformation engendered by this flame must give no pain to the soul which cannot be true except in the beatific vision where this flame is delightful love" (Canticle 39:14). God is a consuming fire (Deut 4:24) and his power will always cause some pain but in the next life he is both 'consummator and restorer'. In the next life God will "consummate the intellect with his wisdom and the will with his love" (39:14).

John wrote 'The Living Flame of Love' for a laywoman, Doña Ana de Peñalosa. Doña Ana was a Segovian who became a widow in 1579. She lived in Granada and housed the discalced Carmelite for seven months when they were in the process of making a foundation in the city. The prioress of the convert was Ana de Jesús for whom John had written the Spiritual Canticle. In 1582 John began to give Doña Ana spiritual direction and he wrote 'The Living Flame of Love' for her. The fact the Living Flame was written for a laywoman shows us that the life of contemplation is meant for all. As the documents of Vatican II (see Lumen Gentium, no. 40) remind us, we are all called to holiness. We are called to union with God.

John began by telling the readers (and Doña Ana) of the need for recollection. Then when the Spirit comes we should produce flames of love in our lives (Prologue 2-3). He uses the image of the wood in the fire here. "Although the fire has penetrated the wood, transformed it, and united it with itself, yet as this fire grows hotter and continues to burn, so the wood becomes more incandescent and inflamed, even to the point of flaring up and shooting out flames from itself" (Prologue 3). The soul is inwardly transformed in the fire of love and elevated by the love so that it is not merely united to the fire, but produces within it a living flame (Prologue 4).

The 'Living Flame of Love' is the Holy Spirit who has transformed the soul in terms of giving it the habit of charity and in producing acts of love. The flame is living because it makes the soul live in God and it is a flame because "it wounds the soul with the tenderness of God's love... in its deepest centre (Flame 1:7-8). John speaks of the deepest centre of the soul where the soul meets God. The Holy Trinity inhabit such a soul. The soul's love is enkindled through the habitual union of love like glowing embers and through the active union of active love like flames shooting from the embers (Flame 1:16).

Here there are parallels with the Canticle (36-40) but John adds a few more details. He speaks of the veils that must be removed before we attain perfect union with God (Flame 1:29). The first is the temporal veil of creatures; the second is the natural veil of our inclinations and operations, while the third is the sensitive veil of union of body and soul. The first two veils must be removed to attain union in this life. The third will only be fully removed when we are in Heaven.

In the second stanza of the Flame John uses the image of cautery/wound, hand, touch to expand on the role of the three persons of the Trinity. He says:

"Thus the hand, the cautery, and the touch are in substance the same. The soul applies these terms to the Persons of the Trinity because of the effect each Person produces.... The first is the delightful wound. This it attributes to the Holy Spirit, and hence it calls him a sweet cautery. The second is the taste of eternal life. This it attributes to the Son, and thus calls him a delicate touch. The third is transformation, a gift by which all debts are fully paid. This it attributes to the Father, and hence calls him a gentle hand."

(Flame 2:1)

The cautery of the Holy Spirit burns the soul in proportion to its desire. It is of infinite power but still is experienced as sweet because it enlarges or delights the soul and does not destroy it (Flame 2:2-5). The very cautery that causes it [the wound], cures it and by curing it, causes it. "As often as the cautery touches the wound of love, it causes a deeper wound of love and thus the more it wounds, the more it cures and heals... to such an extent that the entire soul is dissolved into a wound of love" (Flame 2:7). This cautery is a "touch only of divinity on the soul, without any intellectual or imaginative form or figure" (Flame 2:8).

He goes on to say: "God sometimes permits an effect to extend to the bodily senses in the fashion in which it existed interiorly, the wound and the sense appear outwards, as happened when the seraph wounded St. Francis" (Flame 2:13). St. Paul spoke of bearing Christ's wounds in his body (Gal 6:17). He was referring to his union with Christ and the sufferings he endured. In the case of St. Francis, he contemplated the figure of Christ crucified and his union with the suffering Christ was seen in his body as the stigmata. For St. Francis it appeared that the whole world was bathed in a sea of love and he had universal compassion for all.

The gentle hand and the delicate touch are the merciful and omnipotent Father and his action through the Son (Flame 2:16). The Father's hand is powerful enough to have created the world but can at the same time be gentle and healing in his dealings with the soul. John can say "Your only-begotten Son, O merciful hand of the Father, is the delicate touch by which you touched me with the force of your cautery and wounded me" (Flame 2:16). Those who withdraw and pray in solitude will come to know this gentle presence. John says "The more you dwell permanently within them, the more you touch them, so that the substance of their soul is now refined, cleansed and purified... As a result you hide them in the secret of your face, which is your Word" (Flame 2:17).

John warns we must be prepared to carry our cross, be placed on it and drink gall and vinegar as Christ did in order to obtain life for us (Flame 2:28-30). However all the souls operations are now in God and suffering is not the end. Just as God raised Jesus from the dead so now he raises us to be a new creation.

In Stanza 3 and its commentary John spends a long time discussing the damage the confessor who does not understand interior prayer can do (Flame 3:28-67). The great figures of the Old Testament (Moses, David and others) all had knowledge of the divine lamps John speaks of in Stanza 3. With poetic license he describes them as water of the Spirit (citing Song 4:15, Ps 46:4, Acts 2:3, Ezek 36:25-27). The splendour of these lamps of fire are the 'loving acts of knowledge' that God sends into the soul so that the soul becomes air within the flame, that is it is inflamed with love (Flame 3:9). In the Sayings of Light and Love John says: "You will not take from me, my God, what you once gave me in your Son, Jesus Christ, in whom you gave me all I desire" (no. 26) and in no. 27, he speaks of possessing all things in Christ: "Mine are the heavens and mine is the earth. Mine are the nations, the just are mine, and mine the sinners. The angels are mine, and the Mother of God, and all things are mine."

John speaks about the deep caverns of feeling. John sees that our current state must be transformed. John seems to mean that the soul has depths, that it possesses within itself an image of the Divinity. These make the soul open to the activity of God. The profound caverns are seen as voids waiting for God "since anything less than the infinite fails to fill them" (Flame 3:18). The suffering of the caverns can be intense as God disposes the soul for full union (Flame 3:68). Then John sums up the transforming union of love (Flame 3:78-85). The reciprocal love between God and the soul means they have all things in common, just as the Son told the Father "All my goods are yours and yours are mine" (Jn 17:10).

The commentary on Stanza 4 is very short. The bridegroom awakens love "in the very centre and depth of my soul, which is its pure and intimate substance" (Flame 4:3). The soul now knows all creatures through God.

Because we are now joined to God, "our awakening is an awakening of God" (Flame 4:9). We can love all things in God.

Thérèse of Lisieux was inflamed with the love of God that John spoke about. She found her vocation when she read Paul's first letter to the Corinthians chapter 13. She said "I will be love in the heart of the Church" (MS B, 3 V°). She read in John's Canticle: "For a little of this pure love is more precious to God and the soul, and more beneficial to the church, even though it seems to be doing nothing, than all these other works put together" (Canticle 29:2). She wrote a poem called 'Living on Love'.

> Living on Love is living on your life,
> Glorious King, delight of the elect.
> You live for me, hidden in a host.
> I want to hide myself for you, O Jesus!
> Lovers must have solitude,
> A heart-to-heart lasting night and day.
> Just one glance of yours makes my beatitude.
>   I live on Love! . . .

Later on in the poem she sees how to live on love is to wipe the face of the wounded Jesus. She says:

> Living on Love is wiping your Face,
> It's obtaining the pardon of sinners.
> O God of Love! May they return to your grace,
> And may they forever bless your Name . . . .
> Even in my heart the blasphemy resounds.
> To efface it, I always want to sing:
> "I adore and love your Sacred Name.
>   I live on Love! . . ."   (PN 17:11)

She described earlier how she must bring God's love to the darkness of hearts that do not know love. She said:

> Living on Love is sailing unceasingly,
> Sowing peace and joy in every heart.
> Beloved Pilot, Charity impels me,
> For I see you in my sister souls.

Charity is my only star.
In its brightness I sail straight ahead.
I've my motto written on my sail:
    "Living on Love."   (PN 17:8)

Following her teacher John of the Cross she now begins to speak of the dying of love (see Flammes D'Amour, p. 159f). In the final verse she says:

Dying of Love is what I hope for.
When I shall see my bonds broken,
My God will be my Great Reward.
I don't desire to possess other goods.
I want to be set on fire with his Love.
I want to see Him, to unite myself to Him forever.
That is my heaven ... That is my destiny:
    Living on Love!!! ...   (PN 17:15)

This 'dying of love' now enters her vocabulary. She is filled with love and wishes others to experience this love too. She also begins to use terms like 'escalator' or lift - she could not use the harsh road of asceticism, she had to depend on Jesus alone to bring her to the heights of love. She gave herself to the work of the Holy Spirit in love - He is the 'living flame of love'.

In the Sayings of Light and Love, John speaks of the meaning of the things he has received from God. Number 60 of the sayings goes as follows: "When evening comes, you will be examined in love. Learn to love as God desires to be loved and abandon your ways of acting."

Chapter 6

Two Castles:

The image of how one is in contemplation is wonderful. However it can often seem like an unattainable goal. People can experience life as empty, meaningless without any rhyme or reason. The work one does can seem futile and unrewarding. There is a pain deep in the heart of existence. I know that pain, the pain of loneliness, loss and the apparent loss of God. One writer who speaks to this pain is Franz Kafka (+1924). He was a German-speaking Bohemian Jewish novelist and short story writer. He wrote about isolated protagonists faced by bizarre, surrealistic predicaments and incomprehensible social-bureaucratic powers. He explores alienation, existential anxiety, guilt and absurdity. The term Kafkaesque has entered the English language. Kafka was born in Prague, the capital city of Bohemia, then part of the Austro-Hungarian Empire, today part of the Czech Republic. He died in 1924 at the age of 40 from tuberculosis.

The Castle:

This was one of Kafka's works that was published after his death. It is an allegorical novel, published as Das Schloss in 1926. The setting for the novel is a village dominated by a castle. Time seems to have stopped in the wintry landscape and nearly all the scenes occur in the dark. K, the unnamed protagonist, arrives in the village claiming to be a land surveyor, appointed by the castle authorities. His claim is rejected by the village officials and the novel recounts K's efforts to gain recognition from an elusive authority. HIs assistants provide comical relief, rather than any assistance. Klamm, a castle superior, proves utterly inaccessible. K challenges the petty, arrogant officials and the villagers. At the end, when K dies, notification arrives from the Castle recognising him. This novel has echoes in many of our lives.

The Castle is Kafka at his most powerful. The reader is presented with a series of frustrations, K trying again and again to progress his work, but never moving beyond the Castle's snowy environs. The novel begins with K's arrival in the village that lies in the shadow of the Castle:

> "It was late in the evening when K arrived. The village was in deep snow. The Castle hill was hidden, veiled in mist and darkness, nor was there a glimmer of light to show a castle was there. On the wooden bridge leading from the main road to the village, K stood for a long time gazing into the illusory emptiness above him."[1]

The next morning he sees the Castle above him "clearly defined in the glittering air" (p. 11), but K is "disappointed at the Castle; it was after all only a wretched-looking town, a huddle of village houses, whose sole merit, if any, lay in being built of stone; but the plaster had long since flaked off and the stone seemed to be crumbling away" (11-12).

After viewing the Castle, K thinks of his hometown, and

> "in his mind compared the church tower at home with the tower above him. The church tower, firm in line, soaring unfalteringly to its tapering point, topped with red tiles and broad in the roof, an earthly building – what else can men build? – but with a loftier goal than the humble dwelling-houses, and a clearer meaning in the muddle of everyday life"
> (p. 12)

The Castle, like the church, seems to hold out hope for some meaning, but as the novel progresses this hope is dashed.

The mood created by Kafka is understood at a deep level. He destabilises us by writing about the familiar, the banality of ordinary existence, but disguising it so it appears to us as a strange dream or fairytale.[2] When we close the pages we are returned to reality aware of all the feelings of hopelessness that we tend to shut out with our daily working lives: Kafka

---

[1] Franz Kafka, The Castle (New York: 1965).
[2] William Burrows, Winter Read, The Guardian, 22 Dec 2011.

does write about bureaucracy and unfair process. His major themes however are aloneness, pain, the longing for human companionship, the need to be respected and understood, sex, and the struggle for meaningful existence. We are forced into confrontation with human need and often the hurt caused when our human needs are not met. We live in a lonely world where there is little respect and understanding, where there is much abuse. This is a novel for the darkest days of winter. Kafka takes us away from our own lives, with its stresses and secret desolations, only to return us, shattered, to a new reality in which we must confront those areas of our lives we would rather forget about. Kafka's characters are, for me, my pain made incarnate. In naming our pain we can come to self-acceptance. This can be the beginning of healing and open the door for us to come to find God deep within ourselves. The Interior Castle of St. Teresa, which we met earlier, provides us with an antidote to the feelings of hopelessness of Kafka's Castle. Our experience of Kafka's Castle may be compared to John of the Cross's Dark Night of the Soul.

Teresa of Avila:

Teresa found herself drifting in life and this was to lead her to a "second" conversion. She was born in Avila on March 28, 1515, the daughter of Alonso Sanchez de Capeda and his second wife, Doña Beatriz de Ahumada. Modern studies have discovered her Jewish roots.[3]

Teresa's *Life*, like Augustine's *Confessions*, gives us her own perspective on her childhood, adolescence, and early adulthood. The comparison with Augustine is important, because we know that this was one of the books that deeply influenced her. The Confessions (up to the beginning of book 11) were published in Spanish in 1554 and were soon read by Teresa. This is how she describes the effect the book had on her:

> As I began to read the *Confessions*, it seemed to me I saw myself in them. I began to commend myself very much to this glorious saint. When I came to the passage where he speaks of his conversion and read how he heard that voice in the garden

---

[3] For a biography of Teresa and the background to her 'Life' see Bernard McGinn, Mysticism of the Golden Age of Spain (New York: 2017) p. 124-135.

[*Conf.* 8.12.29], it only seemed to me, according to what I felt in my heart, that it was I the Lord called. I remained for a long time totally dissolved in tears and feeling within myself utter distress and weariness.

Teresa goes on to speak of the difficulty she had in giving up her old false self before coming into full possession of her new self dependent on God. She says, "Dear God, what a soul suffers and what torments it endures when it loses its freedom to be its own master! I am astonished now that I was able to live in such a state of torment!" Nonetheless, from the perspective of the transformed Teresa now writing of her former self, she concludes, like Augustine, with an act of confession (*confessio laudis* – confession of praise): "God be praised, who gave me the life to forsake such utter death! (Life 9:7-8).

Thus Teresa relives Augustine's experience of being turned (*convertere*) to God, although here the divine instrument is the text of Augustine and not the voice of the child in the garden. Like Augustine, Teresa is now telling the story of God's work in her life. She participated in the common prayer of the community, observed the rules, and even practiced interior prayer, if half-heartedly. Her devotion to mystical prayer emerged early. In 1538, while staying with her uncle Pedro, she read Francisco Osuna's *Third Spiritual Alphabet*, the bible of the prayer of recollection. Teresa says, "And so I was very happy with this book and resolved to follow that path with all my strength. Since the Lord had already given me the gift of tears and I enjoyed reading, I began to take time out for solitude, to confess frequently, and to follow that path, taking the book as my master." Through reading Osuna, and later Bernardino de Laredo's *Ascent of Mount Sion*, Teresa came in contact with mystical *recogimiento* and its deep rooting in the "Affective Dionysianism" of the late Middle Ages, in which ecstatic love unites the soul to God above all understanding. This was to be a major source of her own later writing. But while Teresa had begun to practice mystical prayer at a fairly early stage, she did so on her own terms, not on God's. Nonetheless, some special graces were given her. For example, in *Life* 4.7 she mentions brief moments of being given the "prayer of quiet" (an ambiguous term across her writings) and even talks about attaining some kind of "union" with God. Christ appeared to her, possibly in 1539, but in a judgmental way, threatening her about a bad friendship that was leading her astray (*Life* 7.6). The devil tempted her to give up mental prayer for some time, but with the advice of the Dominican Vicente Barrón she took it up again (*Life* 7.17). Teresa wanted to devote herself wholeheartedly to interior prayer and love of Jesus, but she continued to oscillate and waver. Throughout the chapters dealing with her first twenty years in the convent (*Life* 4-8), she was reliving the dilemma Augustine described in book 8 of the *Confessions*, the agony of the divided soul who knows what is the right thing to do but who cannot really do it wholeheartedly because of its dependence on self, not on divine grace. Conversion comes from God, not from one's own efforts. God won through Teresa's weakness.

From this perspective chapters 9-10, which close off the first section of the *Life*, take on a central importance. In chapter 9 Teresa recounts the events (probably in Lent of 1554) that have been described as her "second conversion" (i.e., after the first conversion to the religious life). The first event was seeing a statue of Jesus as the familiar medieval "Man of Sorrows" (*Ecce Homo*), an object that the Encarnación had borrowed for Lent (Life 9.1-3). Teresa testifies to the emotional reaction she experienced in fully realising Christ's sufferings for her. Even more important was the effect this had in helping her put her trust in God and not in herself. She says: "I was very distrustful of myself and placed all my trust in God. I think I said I would not rise from there until he granted what I was begging from him" (*Life* 9.3).

Let us now turn to the *Life* itself and what it has to tell us about the first forty years of Teresa's life as a child, young woman, and an ordinary nun. Teresa's purpose in the first nine chapters of the *Life* is to give us a picture, not unlike Augustine's *Confessions*, of indolent self-reliance as the weight holding the soul back from God, even when it really desires to do God's will. Teresa's childhood pious desires, such as her attempt to go off to Muslim lands to be martyred for Christ (*Life* 1.4) help paint a picture of someone raised in a fervent religious environment, with many good intentions, but unable to follow through. The unspecified sin of her teenage relationship to a cousin (*Life* 2.2, 6-7 [we are not told exactly what this was]) is presented as an offence both against God's law and against the Spanish conception of female honour. In the manner of many saints, Teresa seizes on what may seem like small things (e.g., her vanity, her liking of secular literature, etc.) as evidence of her deep sinfulness. Nevertheless, she was quite pious in the conventional Spanish manner, so it makes perfect sense that, after some hesitation, she entered the Carmelite convent of the

Encarnación in Avila in 1535. The Encarnación was a large community and observant in its way, but it did mirror contemporary Spanish society and the rather relaxed life of the unreformed Carmelite houses. As Doña Teresa de Ahumada, Teresa was among the wealthier nuns with a private room and many privileges. She fulfilled her religious duties but also took advantage of her status to receive guests in the convent parlour and to spend long periods outside the walls, especially when ill. Teresa wanted to have it both ways, that is, as she once put it, "to practice prayer and to live for my own pleasure" (*Life* 13:6) – the divided will that Augustine portrayed so well in *Confessions* book 8.

Chapters 3–8 of the *Life* feature many descriptions of Teresa's often serious illnesses during these twenty years (1535-1555). These include fainting fits, severe fevers and pains, and even a paralysis that brought her near death and from which she did not recover for three years (ca. 1539-42; see *Life* 6.2, 6–8). In the nineteenth century these accounts, as well as her subsequent descriptions of ecstatic raptures and diabolic assaults, led to Teresa being named "the patron saint of hysterics". Hysteria has gone the way of other pseudo-illnesses, but attempts to account for the nun's medical problems and her detailed descriptions of her bodily and spiritual paranormal states continue to attract interest. Were her early illnesses, including the long paralysis, psychosomatic reactions to her interior struggles over her dissatisfaction with her fragmented inner life? It is hard to know, especially when so many competing diagnoses have been offered. Despite their troubling nature, there seems to be a growing recognition that Teresa's illnesses, diabolical attacks, and ecstasies were not expressions of some degenerative pathology but were side effects of the transformation of her consciousness from the selfish ego of Doña Teresa de Ahumada to Teresa de Jesús, the new mystical self grounded in God. As she became more and more rooted in contemplation, Teresa was better able to put her bad health in perspective. As the says in *Life* 13.7: "I have seen clearly that on very many occasions, though I am in fact very sickly, it was a temptation from the devil or from my own laziness – for afterward when I wasn't so cared for and pampered, I had much better health."[4]

For two decades Teresa lived as an average nun in the Encarnación, better than many we may suppose, and worse than others, at least in praise

[4] McGinn, op. cit., p. 131.

(*confessio laudis*), confession of sin (*confessio peccati*), and confession of faith/truth (*confessio fidei/veritatis*). Again like Augustine, Teresa's account of God's turning her from sin to grace is the story of a process, with the reading of the Confessions as one decisive moment in a series of graced interventions. Making public her account was not her own decision, she says, but is presented as an act of obedience to her confessors. Since she is no longer her old self-willed self but is now a mystical self transformed by God's love, Teresa is obeying God through her confessors. The point is underlined in chapter 23, when she returns to the story of her post-conversion life after some chapters discussing prayer: "This is another, new book from here on – I mean another new life. The life dealt with up to this time was mine; the one I lived from the point where I began to explain these things about prayer is the one God lived in me" (*Life* 23:1). At the end of the Life she reiterates the point. Addressing her confessor, the Dominican García de Toledo, who had commanded the work to be written, she hopes that the book "may bring someone to praise God, if only once." Hence, she asks García and three other confessors/advisors to pass judgement on it, and if it is badly done, they can blame her; but "if it is well done, they are good and learned men, and I know they will see where it comes from and praise him [i.e., God] who spoke it through me (*y albarán a quien lol ha dicho por mí*)" (*Life* 40:34).

Teresa had drifted. It was only when she looked at the figure of the wounded Christ (the *Ecce Homo*) that she could see she had not lived an authentic life and this led to her second conversion, as she called it. She became more fully herself in giving herself totally to Christ. She began to see she was no longer in charge but she was now God's. This was a big step for Teresa who had always been the one in charge.

Re-visiting Teresa's Castle:

We met Teresa's Castle earlier. We now look at the sixth and seventh rooms or mansions more closely. The King lives at the centre of our being. The 'Interior Castle' is an allegorical account of the person's journey inward.

In the sixth dwelling place the soul is led through increasing unitive encounters with God. Teresa describes the way the soul is touched by God. The soul and God begin to make real the capacity of the soul. The soul is created "in the image and likeness of God" (Gen 1:26). This image is restored in a loving relationship with God. Teresa sees the sixth dwelling place as the place "where the soul is now wounded with love for its spouse" (Castle VI:1:1). Teresa comes to know herself and God. She discovers who she truly is when she meets God. The "wound of love", which Teresa speaks of is the love she experiences in her soul. In the Song of Songs we read: "I adjure you, O daughters of Jerusalem, if you find my beloved, tell him I am sick with love (Song 5:8). Teresa has a mutual loving relationship with God. She can say: "My beloved is mine and I am his" (Song 2:16). For Teresa the wound of love is the opening created in the soul for God's communication to the soul. "From this union comes its fortitude" (Castle VI:1:2). The wound shows increased relational identity and new potentiality. We are aware of what we were (Teresa in her Life) and we die to our past and allow ourselves to be transformed by love in the present. Teresa says that our encounters can contain the forms of visions, locutions and raptures and she writes about these in detail.

The soul's desire for union with God is purified and its focus intensified. The soul feels a deep longing for union with God, a desire that intensifies with its brief encounters with God:

> But the Spouse does not look at the soul's great desires that the betrothal take place, for He still wants it to desire this more, and He wants the betrothal to take place at a cost; it is the greatest of blessings. And although everything is small when it comes to paying for this exceptional benefit, I tell you, daughters, that for the soul to endure such delay it needs to have that token or pledge of betrothal that it now has. O God help me, what interior and exterior trials the soul suffers before entering the seventh dwelling place!
>
> (VI:1:1)

The soul's restlessness is akin to the intense search of the bride in the Song of Songs as she wanders searching for the bridegroom in Song of Songs 3:1-3 and again in 5:5-8. She moves into a phase of self-abandonment to God. She describes love arising in the soul: "This action of love is so powerful that the soul dissolves with desire,..." (VI:2:4)

The soul can encounter both internal and external trials. The internal trials go to the very heart of the person's identity while the external trials teach it to seek its consolation only in God. When Teresa describes the external trials that the soul experiences (VI:1:3-5) she reveals how the soul has turned the critical corner of de-personalising life's challenges and seeing all things that would have been a crisis before as a grace-filled opportunity to learn:

> This is an amazing truth. Blame does not intimidate the soul but strengthens it. Experience has already taught it the wonderful gain that comes through this path. It feels that those who persecute it do not offend God; rather that His Majesty permits persecution for the benefit of the soul. And since it clearly experiences the benefits of persecution, it acquires a special and very tender love for its persecutors. It seems to it that they are greater friends and more advantageous than those who speak well of it.
>
> (VI:1:5)

The soul has to struggle with the gossip, envy and strife in her life. Now her relationship with God is all-consuming and this changes her attitude to greed, envy and strife. In Kafka's Castle the soul was broken by these experiences, but in Teresa's Castle she will not be overcome and love will win out. It will give her a new identity.

In chapter 4 Teresa discusses rapture of being drawn out of one's senses. It is a type of final purification, a more intense experience of burning from the spark of love

> It seems that His Majesty from the interior of the soul makes the spark we mentioned increase, for He is moved with compassion in seeing the soul suffer so long a time from its own desire. All burnt up, the soul is renewed like the phoenix, and one can devoutly believe that its faults are pardoned. Now that it is so pure, the Lord joins it with Himself, without anyone understanding what is happening except these two.
>
> (VI:4:3)

The soul is entering into the deep reality of the Song of Songs. Teresa describes the soul as being wounded with love. She describes this love as a form of cauterisation, noting "it's as though from this fire enkindled in the brazier that is my God a spark leapt forth and so struck the soul that the flaming fire was felt by it" (VI:2:4). The soul receives the fire but cannot enkindle it. Teresa goes on in the next part to discuss how to discern what is from God and what is not. This leads her to describe the experience of rapture above. The soul is completely thrown out of its ordinary routine and perspective on life and its meaning. It is radically disorientated only to find itself reorientated in a loving union with God. It now establishes a deep trust in God and the way God works with the soul. She surrenders to his guidance and she co-operates with God's way of dealing with her. Teresa describes this process of total trust, telling the soul who has "with such willingness offered everything to God" to "understand that it in itself has no longer any part to play". The soul must be "determined now to do no more than… abandon itself into the hands of the one who is all-powerful, for it sees that the safest thing to do is to make a virtue of necessity" (VI:5:2). Teresa uses the metaphor of the soul being a helpless ship, mercilessly tossed about in a tempest:

> Here this great God, who holds back the springs of water and doesn't allow the sea to go beyond its boundaries, lets loose the springs from which the water in this trough flows. With a powerful impulse, a huge wave rises up so forcefully that it lifts high this little bark that is our soul. A bark cannot prevent the furious waves from leaving it where they will; nor does the pilot have the power, nor do those who take part in controlling the ship.
>
> (VI:5:3)

This is an awesome experience in the deeper sense of the word, so "great courage is necessary" (VI:5:4).

The joy of love enables the soul to achieve this abandon. Teresa tells us that the experience of love radiates from the soul out to others: "It seems it has found itself and like the father of the prodigal son, it would want to prepare a festival and invite all because it sees itself in an undoubtedly safe place, at least for the time being" (VI:6:10). At the beginning of chapter 7 Teresa asserts that the soul's joy at the experience of love and deeper union reinforce its understanding of the fragile state of humanity. She in her journey had come to know herself, her weaknesses but in Jesus she found herself accepted, loved, forgiven and was now living a new life enkindled by love. In accepting herself the soul can accept others. Teresa tells us that sins are "always… alive in the memory and this is a heavy cross" (VI:7:2).

The memory of first failures enables the soul see how much greater is the love that is God. In the face of God's love and compassion, the soul learns compassion towards itself and then extends this to others. Teresa tells us to focus on the embodied life of Christ. In chapter 8 Teresa describes the effects of the habit of contemplation. The soul lives in the presence of the incarnate God. Teresa says "the soul will feel Jesus Christ, our Lord, beside it. Yet it doesn't see Him, neither with the eyes of the body nor with those of the soul. This is called an intellectual vision. I don't know why". Teresa shared this presence but she could not understand it as a vision "since she could not see anything" (Castle VI:8:2). She describes her experiences as experiences of transformative companionship. She writes:

> This continual companionship gives rise to a most tender love for His Majesty, to some desires even greater than those mentioned to surrender oneself totally to His service, and to a great purity of conscience because the presence at its side makes the soul pay attention to everything. For even though we already know that God is present in all we do, our nature is such that we neglect to think of this. Here the truth cannot be forgotten, for the Lord awakens the soul to His presence beside it.…[T]he soul goes about almost continually with actual love for the One who it sees and understands is at its side.
>
> (VI:8:4)

The Father and the Son are present to the soul by the Holy Spirit (Jn 14:16-23). By the power of the Holy Spirit the soul shares in the love between Father and Son and lives from that place.

In Teresa's mansions there is no door between the sixth and seventh mansion. One leads naturally into the other. It is in the seventh mansion that we find where God lives: "For just as in heaven so in the soul His Majesty must have a room where he dwells alone. Let us call it another heaven" (Castle VII:1:3). Like the cellar in the Song of Songs (Song 1:1-4), the soul must be brought into its innermost chamber. The union between God and the soul is, in the seventh dwelling place, a non-ecstatic, permanent experience of God's indwelling presence. The revelations of God now flow into the soul. Union is no longer fleeting. The soul now dwells in the ongoing presence of God. It is both a resting with the divine and moving with the divine. Teresa says:

In this seventh dwelling place the union comes about in a different way: Our good God now desires to remove the scales from the soul's eyes and let it see and understand, although in a strange way, something of the favour he grants it. When the soul is brought into that dwelling place, the Most Blessed Trinity, all three Persons, through an intellectual vision, is revealed to it through a certain representation of the truth.

(VII:1:6)

The soul is prepared for this revelation of God's nature first through an "enkindling of the spirit" and then through an experience of God as Trinity. This is done "through an admirable knowledge the soul understands as a most profound truth that all persons are one substance and one power and one knowledge and one God alone". The knowledge of the Trinity is not abstract even though "it knows in such a way that which we hold by faith, it understands, as we say, through faith" for at this part:

All three Persons communicate themselves to it, speak to it, and explain those words of the Lord in the Gospel: that He and the Father and the Holy Spirit will come to dwell with the soul that loves Him and keeps His commandments.

(VII:1:6)

Teresa goes on to say: "the soul finds itself in this company every time it takes notice" (VII:1:9). It is introduced to the reality in such a way it participates in this very reality of God:

Each day this soul becomes more amazed, for these Persons never seem to leave it anymore, but it clearly beholds, in the way that was mentioned, that they are within it. In the extreme interior, in some place very deep within itself, the nature of which it doesn't know how to explain, because of a lack of learning, it perceives this divine company.

(VII:1:7)

The soul now becomes preoccupied with the reality of God and working in his service (Castle VII:1:8). The seventh dwelling place or mansion is the realisation of the "then" of Paul's famous passage: "For we now see in a mirror dimly, but then face to face. Now I know in part: then I shall understand fully, even as I have been fully understood" (1 Cor 13:12). We have been loved and accepted by God and now in the seventh mansion we live in that love. We live in the union of love between Father and Son by the power of the Holy Spirit.

God is present at the centre of the soul. Teresa speaks of "extreme delight" and "sublime favour". She says: "I can only say that the Lord wishes to reveal for that moment, in a more sublime manner than through any spiritual vision or taste, the glory of heaven" (VII:2:3). The soul is one with God in such a way that "just as those who are married cannot be separated, He doesn't want to be separated from the soul" (VII:2:3). Unlike the sixth mansion where there are times when the soul and God can be separate, now "the soul always remains with God in that centre" (VII:2:4). Teresa goes on to say:

> In the spiritual marriage the union is like what we have when rain falls from the sky into a river or fount; all is water, for the rain that fell from heaven cannot be divided or separated from the water of the river. Or it is like what we have when a little stream enters the sea; there is no means of separating the two.
> (VII:2:4)

Now the life of the soul is God. Now it is led into a more selfless world and care for the other is permanent.

> For if it is with God very much, as is right, it should think little of itself. All its concern in taken up with how to please God more and how or where it will show God that love it bears God. This is the reason for prayer, my daughters, the birth always of good works, good works.
> (VII:4:6)

The soul receives impulses of love that flow from the soul's life with God. These come from the gentle presence of God who lives at the centre of the soul permanently (VII:4:8-9). "So in this temple of God, in this His dwelling place, He alone and the soul rejoice together in the deepest silence" (VII:4:11). We become partners with God in his activity. Teresa says:

In sum, my Sisters, what I conclude with is that we shouldn't build castles in the air. The Lord doesn't look so much at the greatness of our works as at the love with which they are done. And if we do what we can, His Majesty will enable us each day to do more and more.

(VII:4:15)

Teresa ends by encouraging readers to delight "in this interior castle" very often, for the door is always open and there are untold riches to be found in this life of union. She promises: "Once you get used to enjoying this castle, you will find rest in all things, even those involving much labour, for you will have the hope of returning to the castle which no-one can take from you" (Epilogue 2). Contemplation of the self in God empowers us to see more of the beauty of God who creates us and the capacity we have for the same kind of loving intimacy that brings goodness into being.

Although no more than seven dwelling places were discussed, in each of these there are many others, below and above and to the sides, with lovely gardens and fountains and labyrinths, such delightful things that you would want to be dissolved in praises of the great God who created the soul in His own image and likeness.

(cf. Epilogue:3)

Teresa knew this world by experience. She wrote for us so that we, too, can find our way "in the interior castle". The world of Kafka describes our pain when we feel divorced from this "interior castle". Teresa, however, tells us that Kafka's castle is not the end but the beginning. She gives us a roadmap to the "interior castle". She has travelled this road and written about it so that we can follow. She tells us, yes, it takes courage because it is counter-cultural, but at the same time she inspires us to seek the kingdom within. We are loved, accepted and forgiven. We need courage to accept this, but it is worth the effort. Teresa has told us so and she knows. "Do you not know that your bodies are temples of the Holy Spirit, who is in you, whom you have received from God." (1 Cor 6:19)

Bibliography

Ahlgren, G., *Entering Teresa of Avila's Castle: A Reader's Companion* (Minneapolis: 2016)

Alexander, Philip S., trans., *The Targum of Canticles*, The Aramaic Bible (Collegeville: MN: 2003)

Armstrong, Regis, J.A. Wayne Hellmen, William J. Short, *Francis of Assisi - The Saint: Early Documents, Vol. 1* (New York: 1991)

Barth, Karl, *Church Dogmatics, III, 2, The Doctrine of Creation* (Edinburgh: 1960)

Beattie, Tina, *The New Atheists: The Twilight of Reason and the War on Religion* (Maryknoll: 2008)

Bergson, Henri, *Creative Evolution* (London: 1911), translated from the French, original title, *L'Évolution Créatrice.*

Bergson, Henri, *La Pensée et le Mouvant* in A. Robinet (ed.), Henri Bergson, Oeuvres (Paris: 1959)

Bergson, Henri, *Le Due Fonti della Morale e della Religione* (Rome-Bari: 1995). This book is a translation of *Les Deux Sources de la Morale et de la Religion* (Paris: 1932)

Bernard, Charles-Andre, *Le Dieu des Mystiques, vol.1* (Paris:1994)

Bernard of Clairvaux, *Sancti Bernardi Opera* (Rome: 1957-1977)

Burrows, William, *Winter Read, The Guardian*, 22 Dec 2011.

Chase, Stephen, *Contemplation and Compassion: The Victorine Tradition* (London: 2003)

Climacus, John, Ladder of Divine Ascent, quoted in Olivier Clement, *The Roots of Christian Mysticism* (New York: 1993)

Crittenden, Lindsey, *The Water Will Hold You: A Skeptic Learns to Pray* (New York: 2007)

Dawkins, Richard, *The God Delusion* (London: 2006)

De Bodin de Galembert, Laurent, *Idée, Idéalisme et Idéologie, Dans les Oeuvres Choisies de Saint Exupéry* (Thesis: Université Paris IV, 2000)

De Osuna, Francisco, *Troisieme abécédaire* (Madrid: 1911)

De Ros, Fidèle, *Le Frère Bernardin de Laredo* (Paris: 1948)

De Waal, Esther, *The Way of Simplicity: The Cistercian Tradition* (London:1998)

Dunn, J.D.G., *The Theology of Paul the Apostle* (Edinburgh: 2006)

Frankl, Viktor, *Man's Search for Meaning* (New York: 1985)

Frankl, Viktor, *The Unconscious God* (New York: 1985)

Gaucher, Guy, *Flammes d'Amour: Jean et Thérèse. L'influence de saint Jean de la Croix dans la vie et les écrits de sainte Thérèse de Lisieux* (Paris: 1996)

Gilson, Etienne, *The Mystical Theology of St. Bernard* (London: 1940)

Green, Deirdre, *Gold in the Crucible: Teresa of Avila and the Western Mystical Tradition* (Shaftesbury: 1989)

Hillesum, Etty, *An Interrupted Life* (New York: 1996)

Imhof, Paul, Harvey D. Egan and Hubert Biallowons, eds., *Faith in a Wintry Season: Interviews and Conversations with Karl Rahner in the last years of his life* (New York: 1990)

Imhof, Paul, and Hubert Biallowons, eds., *Karl Rahner in Dialogue* (New York: 1986)

Jenson, Robert W., *Interpretation: Song of Songs* (Louisville: 2005)

Kafka, Franz, *The Castle* (New York: 1965)

Kavanagh, Kieran, trans., *The Collected Letters of St. Teresa of Avila,* 2 *volumes* (Washington D.C.: 2001)

Kavanagh, Kieran, and Otilio Rodriguez, trans., *The Collected Works of St. Teresa of Avila,* (Washington D.C.: 1976)

Kavanagh, Kieran, and Otilio Rodriguez, trans., *The Collected Works of Saint John of the Cross* (Washington D.C.: 1991)

Kull, Robert, *Solitude: Seeking Wildness in Extremes* (Novato, Ca.: 2008)

Larson, R.P., trans., *Origen, The Song of Songs: Commentary and Homilies, Ancient Christian Writers, vol. 26* (Westminster MD: 1947)

Lev Chadash, Siddur, *Services and Prayers for Weekdays and Sabbaths, Festivals and Various Occasions* (Union of Liberal and Progressive Synagogues: London: 1995)

Martin, Thomas F., *Our Restless Heart: The Augustian Tradition,* (London: 2003)

Matthew, Iain, *The Impact of God: Soundings from St. John of the Cross* (London: 2010)

Maxsein, A., *Philisophia Cordis Das Wesen der Personalität bei Augustus* (Salzburg: 1966)

McGinn, Bernard, *The Foundations of Mysticism* (New York: 1991)

McGinn, Bernard, *The Growth of Mysticism* (New York: 1994)

McGinn, Bernard, *The Flowering of Mysticism: Men and Women in the New Mysticism (1200-1350)* (New York: 1998)

McGinn, Bernard, *The Harvest of Mysticism in Medieval Germany (1300-1500)* (New York: 2005)

McGinn, Bernard, *The Varieties of Vernacular Mysticism (1350-1550)* (New York: 2013)

McGinn, Bernard, *Mysticism in the Reformation (1500-1650)* (New York: 2017)

McGinn, Bernard, *Mysticism in the Golden Age of Spain (1500-1650)* (New York: 2017)

McGrath, Alister, *Scientific Theology*, 3 vols (London: 2003)

McGrath, Alister, and Joanna Collicutt McGrath, *The Dawkins Delusion* (London: 2007)

Murphy, John J., *St. John of the Cross and the Philosophy of Religion: Love of God and the Conceptual Parameters of a Mystical Experience*, *Mystics Quarterly 22* (1996)

Nemeck, Francis Kelly, OMI, and Marie Theresa Coombs, *Contemplation* (Collegeville, MN: 1982)

Nicholl, Donald, *Triumphs of the Spirit in Russia* (London: 1999)

Norris, Richard A., (ed.), *The Song of Songs: Interpreted by Early Christian and Medieval Commentators* (Grand Rapids: 2003)

Nouwen, Henri J.M., *Life of the Beloved* (New York: 1992)

O'Brien, John, *With Thee Tender is the Night* (CreateSpace: 2016)

Payne, Steven, *John of the Cross and the Cognitive Value of Mysticism: An Analysis of Sanjuanist Teaching and its Philosophical Implications for Contemporary Discussions of Mystical Experience*, New Syntheses Historical Library 37 (Dodrecht: 1990)

Pennington, M. Basil, *Lectio Divina: Reviewing the Ancient Practice of Praying the Scriptures* (New York: 1998)

Peers, E. Allison, *The Complete Works of John of the Cross, 3 vols.*, (London: 1935)

Popkin, Richard H, *The Columbia History of Western Philosophy* (Columbia: 2006)

Rahner, Karl, *Theological Investigations, XX* (New York: 1981)

Rahner, Karl, *Gnade als Mitte menschlicher Existenz: Ein Gespräch mit und über Karl Rahner aus Anlaß seines 70. Geburtstages*, in Herausforderung des Christen (Freiburg: 1975)

Schopaneur, Artur, *The World as Will and Representation*, 3 vols., (London: 1883-1886)

Sicari, Antonio Maria, *Il "Divino Cantico"* (Foligno: 2011).

Simon, Maurice, trans., *Song of Songs Rabbah*, Midrash Rabbah (London: 1930)

Simon, Raphael, *The Glory of Thy People: The Story of a Conversion* (New Hope: 1985)

Starr, Mirabai (ed.), *Saint John of the Cross: Devotion, Prayers and Living Wisdom* (Boulder, Co.: 2012)

Starr, Mirabai, *Caravan of No Despair: A Memoir of Loss and Transformation* (Sounds True, Colorado: 2015)

Walsh, Kilian, and Irene M. Edmunds, trans., *The Works of Bernard of Clairvaux, vols. 1-4* (Kalamazoo, MI: 1971-1980)

Van Huyssteen, J. Wentzel, *Alone in the World? Human Uniqueness in Science and Theology* (Gifford Lectures: Grand Rapids, 2006)

Von Balthasar, Hans Urs, Theology and Sanctity, chapter in *Explorations in Theology*, vol. 1. The Word Made Flesh (San Francisco: 1989)

Von Balthasar, Hans Urs, "St. John of the Cross", in *The Glory of the Lord: A Theological Aesthetics, vol. 3, Studies in Theological Style: Lay Styles* (San Francisco: 1986)

Zeitschrift für die Alttestamentliche Wissenschaft (ZATW/ZAW)

Printed in Poland
by Amazon Fulfillment
Poland Sp. z o.o., Wrocław